The Australian Guerrilla:

SNIPING

Ion L. Idriess

ETT IMPRINT
Exile Bay

This edition published by ETT Imprint, Exile Bay 2019

Also by Ion L. Indriess
Horrie the Wog Dog
Prospecting for Gold
Flynn of the Inland
The Red Chief
Nemarluk
The Desert Column

The Australian Guerrilla: Sniping

First published 1942 by Angus & Robertson
Reprinted 1942. Facsimile edition 1999 by
Idriess Enterprises.

Copyright © Idriess Enterprises Pty Ltd 2019

ISBN 978-1-925416-85-5 (paper)
ISBN 978-1-925416-84-8 (ebook)

ETT IMPRINT

PO Box R1906

Royal Exchange NSW 1225

Australia

CONTENTS

.

CHAPTER I
The Real Sniper

The most dangerous individual soldier, and the world's best rifle-shot, is the sniper.

I do not mean the soldier who is a good shot and who is occasionally detached as a "sniper," as is grudgingly done now in most armies. I mean the real sniper, the "lone wolf." He is deadly. He is feared more than the tank, more than the aeroplane. The sniper has ever been a lone wolf, has ever been independent. He is the fighter who has remained unchanged throughout the ages right up to today. In all our mechanized armies, our vast organizations, and titanic movements of massed troops, he is the one man who is independent of them all. He wages his own deadly little war regardless of the movements of battlefields, air fleets, panzer divisions, or armies. And he does it all with everyman's weapon. That weapon was once the club. It developed into the arrow. Now it is the rifle.

The sniper holds his life by his initiative, his wits, even more than by his fearlessness. It is not only his rifle, it is his thought beforehand, added to cunning, which makes him so deadly, even against armies. He can kill where an army cannot. And he can bring down the highest. Many a victorious chief, many fighting kings have fallen to the lone wolf. Many a famous general he has laid low. One of the best of our own Australian generals fell to a sniper at Gallipoli. Several Italian, and some among the best known of the German generals, have already fallen to the Russian snipers during this war. In every war the world has known, the sniper has done his deadly work.

And he needs no vast organization behind him. To a great country like Australia with a tiny population, a single brigade of snipers would be worth more than an army corps. Australia breeds the best snipers in the world, and breeds them in numbers. Many an Australian bush lad has grown up with a rifle in his hands. During the last war we outshot the Turkish snipers, and they were noted among the armies of the world.

For long past I have been advocating the organizing of our born snipers, their offensive power to be used for sniping work only. Perhaps it is not yet too late.

The ambition of every keen rifleman while his country is at war is to be a sniper. I'll tell you all I know about it, but always be eager to learn more. A sniper can be born to the game. On the other hand, he can learn. But he will never become a real sniper unless he develops into an expert. It is a fascinating game he takes on, but one fraught with deadly peril. You become a lone hunter stalking the most dangerous game on earth—armed men, savage because they know you are seeking their lives; deadly because they are watching out for you. Your own life will be always at stake. Hence, never tire of learning more and more about the game. The knowledge that you gain from others will prove of great value. The knowledge you gain from personal experience will complete your education. Never lose your wariness for one moment.

Make up your mind from the start. If you decide to

become a sniper, then the die is cast. No matter whether you are in the regular army or the irregulars, if you decide to become a sniper your life will be in your own hands. There will be no one to help you—unless you are detailed as a sniper in some trench position within your own lines. Inefficiency, carelessness, overconfidence, just one little slip and you are a goner. So, learn all you can before you venture out to shoot men. You must of course be a good shot beforehand. Indeed, an excellent shot; under certain circumstances, for a sniper to miss is fatal.

Before we go into details, get a broad view of the subject. You will then realize what a big (though unrecognized) job has been the sniper's, and what a big job yours can be. There is far more in it than sitting behind a rock waiting for a target to stroll along.

The first sniper did just that, millions of years ago. His enemy was a giant of a fellow, with a tremendous reach and club. The little fellow knew he'd have no chance. So he sat down and frowned and thought—and hit on the brilliant idea of hiding behind a rock and waiting for his enemy to come to the pool to drink. Then, with his little bow and arrow, he shot him while he was bending.

And that was the first Jack the Giant Killer act, the first sniper.

The rule applies perfectly today: Catch your enemy bending. How many of our own *armies* have been caught bending during these last two years!

As I have already indicated, thought is the very life blood of the sniper. From the moment he sets out with his rifle, his wits must be razor keen.

From the first, every tribe has bred its envied snipers. In an age when every tribe had to find its food by the hunt, every man, you'd think, would be a sniper. Not so. It was only the thinkers amongst their craftiest hunters who were the snipers, the hunters who thought beforehand where the game were likely to feed, where the fat bucks would most likely come to water. Those were the men who could plan beforehand just where they would most likely catch their enemy bending. The Boers were a tiny army of trained hunters, every man a rifle-shot from boyhood up. In a body, with their mobility and good rifle-shots, they proved elusive and very dangerous. But the actual out and out snipers amongst them were, fortunately for us, comparatively few.

The northwest frontier of India and Afghanistan is notorious for its snipers. The lone wolf sniper, the deadliest of his species, is comparatively rare. For no matter what a man's job may be, few in that job think really deeply. All of us learn our game, but few become really expert. We have too many other interesting things to think about.

Providing you have the will, there is nothing to prevent you from becoming a sniper when you realize this. Realize that the dangerous sniper is not dangerous merely because he is an excellent shot but because he also thinks deeply; thinks out his own moves both beforehand and on the spur of the moment; thinks out the probable moves of his enemies. He is constantly alert to guard against surprise, constantly seeking to outwit his enemy beforehand.

If you can plan one accurate move ahead of your enemy, you will beat him every time.

The Spartans were exceptional; they were a race of snipers. No Spartan had earned his breakfast who could not shoot it on the wing. They had to be deadly shots to live. A tiny tribe surrounded by numerous enemies, every man had not only to be a dead shot but a sniper with it, able and confident to worm his way into an enemy's camp, put an arrow through the heart of three or four, then slip away in the confusion. It was part of his training in life, all carefully explained beforehand. To succeed, he not only had to be a cool and deadly shot, he had to carefully plan ahead. Otherwise he could not have gotten away with it. If he failed—well, what happened to him does not bear writing about.

It is precisely the same with the successful snipers of today. A few of the real Turkish snipers successfully shot us up in Gallipoli, Sinai, and Palestine. We did the same to them, and eventually beat them at their own game. On an incomparably greater scale, the Russian snipers are playing havoc behind the lines of the German forces today.

Going back to the dim old days, we know the wild guerrilla bands and lone wolf snipers played havoc with the Roman centurions during the years-long struggle to conquer Britain. While slowly but surely Boadicea, with her little army of fighting tribes, was pushed back and back to her last great stand, the snipers were within and behind the Roman lines. Many a centurion stopped an arrow through the heart and knew not whence it came. So it was down through history right to the present day.

But in the massing of huge world armies, the sniper's value has been largely overlooked. I wish we would wake up to his extraordinary value in defence of such a country as ours. Our people and our geographical conditions are ideally suited to mounted and guerrilla warfare, and to sniping. Australia could be a sniper's paradise. If only snipers throughout the continent were organized, they would become of immense value to the regular forces. We have battalions of ready-made snipers waiting for organizing: from the bush, where thousands of men are already excellent shots and used to the conditions of bush and country fighting; from the Rifle Clubs, whose membership before the war was 50,000 men. Many of these spent their weekends for many years preparing themselves exclusively for this army job. Why their rifles have been taken from them at this time of extreme national peril passes my comprehension.

Snipers could be drawn, too, from the army of the civilians, from the regular and irregular troops. But it is essential that they should go through a well-planned course of training for this highly specialized job. The hints contained in this little book should help them.

CHAPTER II
The Cards of the Game

Life to the sniper means to see while not being seen. If he is seen, he does not live long. Study well then how under all circumstances you may become "invisible." By day and by night, on bright days and cloudy days and wet days. On dark nights, moonlit nights, and starlit nights.

Learn how to become invisible while travelling, while walking for miles if necessary. Seems stupid and impossible. Not so. You do not become really invisible but, if you know how, you are invisible to the eyes that seek you.

Use your head and utilize the contours and cover of the country so that the enemy cannot see you. If you cling to one side of a hill while your enemy is scouting along the other, then you are invisible. But if you are silly enough to come up on to the skyline—well, what can you expect?

If you hide in a gully while your enemies pass by, if you successfully hide behind a rock, then you remain invisible to them.

Try to become invisible under all circumstances. See without being seen.

We have 10,000 aids, an army of allies to help us. It depends upon your own grey matter as to how many of these friends you make use of to shield your life. Here are a very,

very few of these friends: yourself, your wits, your eyes, ears, nose, your own movements. The more you work these personal willing allies, the more friends come to your aid: the shelter of rock or tree or gully, the shield of cover in bush or shadow, grass or desert sand. Vanish—but be there and see what is to be seen. You have all the earth to hide you if only you call on her by using your wits, your eyes, your limbs. That earth can hide armies, let alone you. Your wits always come first; they are an army in themselves. You think out your movements first with them, and thus beforehand avoid many dangers. And when the unforeseen happens and critical danger leaps upon you, you instantly use your wits to get out of the mess.

Here's a simple illustration of what I mean. Say that tomorrow you were going out to snipe an enemy outpost. Well, you'd think first: of the safest route by which you could approach the outpost unobserved; of the probable and possible localities in which troops may have filtered; of where an unknown outpost may be stationed. You would plan out the detour, if possible, so as to get completely around the enemy and come up behind him—catch him bending. You would decide whether the best plan would be to start off under cover of the night and ferret out a nice, safe possy with the dawn. Such simple thought would not only ensure your doing your job but it might save your life beforehand. This way:

Had you travelled in the day, then from the moment you left camp you would have run the risk of being seen. Certainly so when you came within field-glass range of the post. You might also have blundered into a wandering patrol, or a lurking sniper, or a bunch of enemy filtered forward. So by thinking first, you may have saved yourself from being shot. The more probabilities and possibilities you think of beforehand, the more prepared you are to guard against them.

That is the simplest illustration. Think well first.

You are going to become a sniper, a fighter operating on your own against whom every enemy hand is raised. You are the lone hunter stalking numerous and very dangerous game. Make your lonely self strong by ever remembering that you really have many friends, friends who will aid you if only you think about them. And the closest of these friends is your own thoughts.

You may be quite alone, but you can outwit a thousand men if you think beforehand, and keep thinking. Remember, too, that thinking develops instinct. Instinct at times can save you quicker than thought.

Instinct dwells in every human being, a relic from the ages when our ancestors were hunters continually being hunted. It was instinct that saved them many a time. It is instinct that warns and saves the animal and bird, the reptile and fish today. At times, it saves us. If a sniper is constantly on the alert, this instinct comes almost instantaneously to the surface, to warn, to caution, and on occasion to urge immediate danger. At such a moment, the body will respond quicker than thought. Instinct is extremely valuable to the sniper. Thought develops it; thought brings it out expectant of danger.

Two other friends are ever with you, eager to be called upon: your eyes. But they cannot help you more than ordinarily unless you encourage them. They can see many things, things you'd never suspect, if only you call upon them. Do that constantly and they will show you things you would never see otherwise.

Try it tomorrow on a shop window in which are very few articles. Glance carefully at it as you pass by. Stop and recall what you have seen. Then return and be staggered by the number of articles you have missed. Try it on a window containing a few coloured materials. Repeat the same procedure. You will find that your colour scheme was all wrong—because you did not use your eyes. You only thought you did.

Such careless "thought" may mean your life in the perilous times ahead.

Look carefully at a tree, then turn away and describe it to yourself. Write down that description. Then turn to the tree and look for the things you did not see. There is a dead limb you had not noticed, and an old mopoke camouflaged up in that big hollow, and another hollow with the bark chewed around the edge. A cockatoo's beak has done that; his wife and babies at this very moment are at home. There are possum scratches on the trunk, too; and a big green tree-frog gawking right at you; and a peewit's nest away out on that slender limb.

Quite apart from peculiarities of the tree itself, such as that grotesque bole which from a distance looks like a man's head, there is quite a lot of life about this tree which you did not notice in your first look: that big mistletoe with the honeysucker busy down at the tendrils, and that lovely staghorn away up there. And there's a big yellow goanna looking down with beady eyes. He certainly sees you. As you examine the tree in detail, you grow more and more surprised at what you did not see. And yet all these things were before your eyes all the time.

Make that tree an object lesson; for if you become a sniper, the things you do not see may one day cost you your life.

Remember that the sniper can be sniped; should the enemy suspect a sniper in the vicinity he will send out other snipers to get him. And those others will try with all their skill to accomplish one thing in particular—to see but not be seen.

Concentrate your sight to seeing things, all things, through your eyes. Expect them to do their job, but remember they are merely organs. There are countless things they will not see unless you direct through them the will to see. Then they become very wide-awake indeed. It is startling how sharp they become when you systematically practise seeing things through them. They grow constantly alert, and the time will come when they will wake you up, trying to tell you things they see which you cannot see. Understand my meaning—your eyes will be warning you of something which mentally you have not contacted through the sight. When your eyes grow to be as quick, as keen, as alert, as suspicious as that, then you really will see, and the length of your career will be enhanced immeasurably.

If your wits, eyes, ears, and body thus grow in cunning together, you will take a lot of catching and will live to snipe for many a day.

CHAPTER III
He Lives Longest Who Learns the Game Best

Your ears are another close friend about whom you know but very little. If you get to know your ears and call upon them, they will hear things that otherwise would pass unnoticed, things that may save your life. The footstep of an enemy coming round the bend, the snap of a twig that can betray a stalker stalking you, a murmur of conversation from a patrol hiding in the grass, a dislodged stone from some careless enemy foot rolling down a gully bank. The sniper who keeps alive develops his hearing, concentrates upon it, and it answers his call.

Your nose is another friend. It can catch a whiff of smoke, some tang of cooking meats from a concealed fire. Or a whiff of tobacco in the night. A trained nose can, under favourable conditions, catch the saltish, sweaty tang from horses. To a sniper travelling across enemy-occupied country by night, his nose is an ally capable under favourable conditions of warning him of danger.

Your body and movements make another personal ally. For, if trained, in a moment you can turn yourself into the stump of a tree, or a hunched-up rock, or some motionless thing that is part of the very earth, or a shadow upon a granite boulder. You can become invisible below water and still breathe, in broad daylight you can vanish in a second into the merest crack in the earth. Even if they have spotted you, you would have wriggled from there before they arrive. Learn the capabilities of your extremely adaptable body. Its speed, its immobility, its vanishing tricks. Its power of squeezing out of many a desperate situation is a priceless gift to the sniper, if only he realizes it. Then he is ready to take advantage of it when the time comes; while at all times the knowledge gives him added confidence.

You must gain confidence; it means a lot. And the only way to gain real confidence is to know that you are a crack shot; that your wits and eyes have developed a most surprising keenness; that you feel fit to tackle any situation. With confidence, you can make your way towards the enemy's lines, can watch his camp in broad daylight from only a few hundred yards away. At night you can creep right into his camp, right up to his very headquarters and watch what's coming and going there, hear the murmur of conversation within. First-class scouts have done that very job in many a war; it was done again and again during the last war; it has been done in this. The very few men who can successfully accomplish such a job are looked upon as the bravest of the brave, almost as supermen. And there is something in it. Still, when it comes to be analysed, he is just a man like you, though a man who has developed his faculties.

In his lonely, desperate job, he has used to the limit all his friends: his wits, his eyes, his ears, his body.

Just according to how much you understand and use your own personal friends, so you can succeed.

In this war, your job quite often may be to penetrate the enemy's lines. Again, to select a possy fronting the enemy where he is infiltrating; to remain hidden and let him pass;

then to deal it out to him. It needs skill and confidence to do that and come back alive.

So, to become a successful sniper you must first of all understand and use your personal friends: yourself, and your wits, eyes, ears, body, and movements.

Besides these personal friends, you also have an army of allies to call upon—if only you understand them and use them. A very few of these allies are the earth, day, night, shadows, illusions, knowledge of country, "bump of locality," camouflage, trees, grass, water, rocks, thunder, lightning, animals, sound, mist, rain, heat, cold, surprise, dismay, unwariness, blissful thinking, observation, memory, and a thousand other important everyday things.

You may wonder what on earth all this has to do with sniping. It has everything. After all, you are merely a man in the world that is ever about you, and your enemies are in the same position. Everything that concerns them concerns you. Your advantage lies only in the fact that you are capable of using everything possible around them and around you to your own advantage.

And your battle action will almost always be the offensive.

Here's one little illustration. You may say, "What on earth has 'blissful thinking' got to do with sniping?"

A lot. When an enemy is a blissful thinker, then he's at your mercy. Much more so if you can anticipate beforehand that he *will* be a blissful thinker. Now, imagine you've been sniping for a week and your possy has become too hot—the enemy is straining every nerve to locate you and, as they are slowly but surely advancing, they will find you in time. You know the country for miles around, so think of one area where there has been very little hot fighting and no real sniping that you know of. Well, your game will be there.

Numbers of the enemy are sure to be prowling here and there somewhere across that country, and they will be "blissful thinkers." They have not been systematically sniped at; they know that the fighting is taking place some miles away; they go about their tasks unwarily, believing that for the time being at least they are safe. Thus they are blissful thinkers and easy marks.

So even blissful thinking can be the ally of the sniper who thinks.

The "offensive" being generally on your side means yet another advantage. For you strike a hidden blow at the moment you choose. Thus the element of surprise is on your side. Get the king hit in first.

If fighting comes to our country, which appears extremely likely, you, the sniper, will thrill to a fascinating life—while it lasts. You can only make it last by thoroughly understanding your game. In truth, you will be "living on your wits." From the moment you start out on your dangerous career, every enemy's hand will be against you; for there is nothing he detests and fears so much as the sniper. He will hunt you with cold fury. Not only will the enemy send a battalion to seek you with bullet and bayonet and grenade and machine-gun, he will turn artillery on to your supposed position; he will try and squash you with a tank; he will even send an aeroplane to try and locate you. If you grow into a dangerous sniper, particularly with a more or less fixed position, he will hunt you with all he's got. Snipers in fixed positions very quickly get to be known. Not their positions, but the knowledge of their presence. A roaming sniper is here today, gone tomorrow, or gone right now. Against it all, you will be one lone man. Use your wits and all your many allies and you can laugh at them. For, after all, it is they who must find that needle in the haystack. The needle leaves no tracks. If you do, then you won't last long.

Your best friend is your wits. The second is Mother Earth. It is for your country you are fighting, and your country will cling to you. The more you use her, the more she will shelter and protect you. Dwell well on that fact. Your great friend is the earth and the countless cloaks she offers you, the protection and cover which is yours on every side. Learn well the earth. Learn that the slightest crease in her face can shield you from a bullet, that a tattered sheet of bark can hide you from prying eyes.

Learn to see at a glance every advantage she offers you and learn how to avail yourself of each. At the same time, realize the fact that while Nature protects you, she betrays your enemy. This is fact only because you have learned more of the earth, of how to use her protection and camouflage better than the enemy. I'll explain it this way: Two men are playing cards. One is a player who knows cards, the other is an ordinary player. That pack of cards gives a perfectly even chance to each player. But the man who knows his cards wins every time.

Thus with the sniper. The more he knows his cards, which are the many phases of nature, the more certainly will he outwit his enemy, not only one man but a whole army of them. Learn well then everything about you, everything you can about country and bush and earth; about all objects; about live things too, whether flesh or vegetable; about rock and clay; about water and wind and anything at all.

For Nature deals the pack, and those are the cards you play with.

And the sniper's stakes are for life or death.

CHAPTER IV
The Art of Hiding

Let us now in more detail learn of these "cards" of yours, the friends Nature offers to help you become and continue to be a successful sniper.

The instinct to hide was Nature's first gift of protection to all her weaker, smaller things, no matter how deadly some might be. The sniper is one of these weaker things, for though he is very deadly, he is weak indeed against an army. Nature taught the hawk to hide while the eagle passed by. She taught the wolf to hide while the tiger passed by. Figures that the astronomers give us of the distances of the stars from the earth are so vast that we cannot understand them. But it would be intensely interesting to know the figures of the countless things that have saved their lives by hiding since the world began.

That is the sniper's first lesson—hiding. He must, of course, be a crack rifle-shot to begin with, but he must also concentrate upon this highly skilled art of hiding.

It is the same now as when the world began. Hide successfully and any danger will pass you by. Hide ineffectually, and you are discovered.

You are beginning to realize now why I wrote that your wits are your friends. Use them to take every advantage of your other "personal friends" and of the countless aids that Nature offers you. Believe me, if you do so you will live a long while as a sniper.

The sniper's possy is his hide-out, his "foxhole," as we called the hiding places of the Turkish snipers. Your life, many a time, will depend on your hide-out. If you have not chosen craftily, you'll never need another.

Study the art of hiding any moment you can. Think a lot about it; practise it. Consider the position and the why and wherefore of the hide-out; the camouflage; and the hide-out in which you would nestle but an hour or so, or for a day.

A sniper, if on active duty away from a settled post, must be instantly prepared to hide throughout any second of the night or day, no matter where he may find himself. He may be dodging through the enemy lines, or be travelling miles away out on a flank, when enemy scouts, patrol, or troops suddenly appear. Instant action, successful hiding, and they can pass within a few feet of him and all is well. But unless he has mastered instant action in the art of hiding, he is a goner. So far as being observed is concerned anyway. If the enemy is some little distance away, he still has a chance, but his life still depends on the same thing—hiding. They are instantly in full chase after him; he will receive no mercy should they catch him. His only chance lies in his wits, his slippery body, and his knack for hiding. Again and again he may hide and eventually get through them and away. But if he cannot successfully and continually hide, he is finished.

How vastly important it is then that he should be able to instantly, successfully hide in the first place! He could just lie doggo until danger gradually passed away. Then the enemy would still be blissfully unaware.

So there is more in hiding than meets the eye. There is life in it.

There may be a small crowd of you keen to become snipers. Get together and discuss this chapter on "hiding." By talking about it, each will broaden the other's view; you will begin to see what a very big thing it is, how your very lives are one day going to depend upon your success in the art of hiding.

Then stroll across to the nearest paddock or bit of bushland. Sit down in a mob, send one of your crowd to go out and hide behind a rock or log a hundred yards or so out to your front. He does so. You cannot see him. You realize that if he were an enemy and you were "blissfully unaware," he could shoot any one of you with ease.

Now, all stand up. Immediately you see a portion of the man's body, or clothes, maybe part of his hat, or his heel or elbow. Now that you have raised yourself to standing height, the hidden man is hidden no longer. He has not understood his job; until he knows it far better, he would not make a sniper's bootlace. Discuss the matter and you will work out the simple fact that the would-be sniper, when he hid, should have known that he must hide in such a way as to be invisible not only to men sitting down two hundred yards away, but to men lying down, kneeling men, standing men, men on horseback or up on a tank, or a motor-cyclist machine-gunner, no matter whether those men were ten yards or a thousand yards away. Otherwise he would not be perfectly safe. In fact, under certain circumstances, he would need to be invisible to a man in a tree.

One among you will notice how his white shirt or black pants stand out so plainly against the grey of log or rock. That will heighten your interest in camouflage, which we will presently discuss. Explain to your mate that he was a "dead bird" immediately when you stood up. Go back to your place, the lot of you, but let him still hide there. If he has hidden so that none of you when standing up can see him, you and he have learned several valuable lessons.

Now, all look around you. Suppose you are a group of enemy troops. You are by no means sure, but are suspicious that an enemy sniper may be somewhere about. There is no sign of him. Very well—scatter and widely encircle that log from two flanks. In no time, one of your number calls out and points. From a slightly higher level of ground he can see part of the sniper behind the log. Simultaneously, another man calls out from the other flank. He is standing up on a log or rock, and from this position he also can see the sniper. Yet another man, looking at a different angle from the rear, can now see the sniper

You all realize that the apparently hidden sniper was all the time visible from half a dozen directions. Under real active service conditions, the enemy could have come from any direction at all. From any one of half a dozen directions would have meant the end of the poor sniper.

CHAPTER V
The Art of Immobility:
How Movement Betrays

From that simple lesson at the end of the last chapter, you have learned how seemingly difficult it is to really hide, to become "invisible." With practise, when you learn to know how, you will find it almost simple.

Now get together again. Hide that man in the same place, but in a different way. Don't be satisfied until he is hidden so well that you cannot see him no matter from what angle you look. You will find that very probably this can be done. Certainly by the aid of camouflage.

When you are all satisfied, you will have thought you've learned a jolly lot. Until one of your number may remark: "Well, we cannot see him. All the same, he has no getaway." Which would be a fact. The sniper is hidden and certainly could get his man, probably two or three. But they would then get him.

A sniper must learn the craft not only of hiding himself from any angle, but also of choosing a possy with a getaway. That is, the lay of the country, or surrounding or nearby cover (should there be any) so that the sniper can slip away unseen if necessary.

A dead sniper is of no use to anyone but the enemy. A live sniper will quickly become dead if he chooses his possy in such a place that he will be seen when he retires, or is forced to retire, from it.

So this simple lesson also teaches you that a hide-out may prove to be a death-trap. Not only must you learn to really hide, but you must learn how to choose a hidden hide-out from which you can escape unseen if circumstances compel. Although you finally hid your man until you could not see him from any angle, his hide-out was an oasis in a bare patch of ground. Had he been forced to move from that position, he would immediately have been seen and could not have got away.

When next you all go out together for a lesson, you will seek a hide-out which gives your man a commanding view of the surrounding country, yet at the same time will lend itself to him quietly slipping away unseen if events demand it.

In hiding, always remember that the great betrayer is "movement." Unguarded movement has betrayed countless men ever since the dim ages. It does so today. Movement has betrayed many a patrol, many a surprise column. It has betrayed armies and battle fleets. Unguarded movement can betray any man today. Learn that fact well. Armies may be fighting around you; there'll be plenty of movement. That does not matter to you so long as you do not betray yourself. Let them fight out their battle. You have your own to fight

The slightest movement can be noticed a surprising distance away by watching eyes. Movement of any sort attracts the eyes, no matter whether they are watching or not. The sway of a bough in the breeze—the flap of a settled bird's wing, the flip of a rabbit's tail, the flight of a butterfly, a shred of bark in the breeze—any movement at all catches the eye.

It is almost unbelievable the instant attraction movement

has for eyes that may be watching. A flick of the hand, a half turn of the head, becomes instantly visible although previously the whole man was invisible. The rule applies at long distance as well as close; for remember that an enemy may be searching for you through field-glasses.

If you have craftily selected your ground and as craftily camouflaged yourself, lie utterly motionless and a man can stare at you from a comparatively few yards away, from a few feet even, and not distinguish you. But move slightly and you are gone. Always remember that incautious movement can betray, even though you are hidden in a possy.

That brings us to the "freeze." You may be out in the open actually walking along when suddenly an enemy comes upon you. There may be a split second left. "Freeze" to the ground, tree, rock, bank, or to anything against which you are.

If there is not a split second left in which to freeze, then freeze into a statue. You may possibly escape by freezing into an immovable man. Men have occasionally escaped an enemy that way by remaining in full view, perfectly still. It depends on your instinct and background, whether you act instantly and naturally, and whether the country—with its contours, trees, rocks, shadows, or landscape—lends itself to your deception. It is possible even to ride past a standing man and, if he never moves, neither rider nor horse may see him.

An enemy in numbers may suddenly come full upon you in such circumstances that your one hope is to bound away and disappear. What saves you then are your wits—if you have learned to use them. Instinct probably will automatically set your limbs in motion.

We will imagine that such an experience befalls you one morning. The day before, it was vaguely known that the enemy were advancing, just feeling their way across the country, but still miles distant. You start out for a bit of shooting. Knowing the country, you have fixed in your own mind the direction in which the enemy are advancing, and the most likely spot where you'd probably meet the first of their advancing forces. The enemy would still be miles away, but you walk ahead cautiously enough for all that, not giving anything away. Perhaps you know a road ahead along which you reckon the enemy will advance, and you are planning a strategic possy on a hillside which commands a bend of that road. At the same time, as you walk along, your wits are keenly alive, working on the probabilities of what may lie ahead, subconsciously working also all around and behind you. Wits, eyes, and ears are all working together. You are walking across country, automatically taking advantage of every sheltering contour and cover—just in case.

At the same time you are subconsciously remembering what lies behind you as you travel, for behind you lies your getaway. Suddenly, the enemy rise at your very feet; you have walked right on them and they actually see you a split second before you see them. But you have wheeled and leaped down a gully and are away before they can shoot

It is only a subconscious mind and action that does that under such circumstances, a mind trained beforehand to act under such a circumstance. You have been taken by utter surprise, but mind and body leap into action and you are saved.

Had you not thought before venturing out, had you not constantly been training your wits, eyes, and ears, then you must have stood staring the second or two necessary for the enemy to recover from their surprise and start blazing away. Even had the first shots missed, they still would have been on your heels as you turned to run. You would hardly have had a fifty-fifty chance. As it is, you have actually disappeared before they fired, let alone leap forward. And as you know the country immediately behind you and they don't, you will get away to fight another day. Wits have saved you— wits that beforehand have planned action to which the body instantly leaps.

And now we come to the freeze in more detail. For the freeze not only enables you to live to fight another day, it enables you to live and fight this day also.

CHAPTER VI
The Art of "Freezing"

The ability to remain motionless–to freeze to earth or tree or rock or to anything near you, or to stand absolutely still on the instant, has often saved a sniper's life.

The enemy eye has failed to pick you up, and it may still miss you if you remain motionless. Perhaps you have walked right upon a party of the enemy at close quarters, or distantly they appear around a bend or over a ridge. If you have a second left to drop to earth or crouch against a bank, do so and instantly become part of that earth, part of that bank.

So long as you do not move an eyelid, they may pass by even within a few yards—within a few feet should your uniform blend with its surroundings. It is the utter immovability that does it, for the unsuspecting eye misses many things—so long as you do not move.

Practise this freeze. It is not quite so simple as it sounds, just to "melt into" whatever is nearest you and remain utterly still. I am emphasizing the freeze because you, as a sniper to be, will be juggling with life and death. A day may well come when the freeze will save you.

To prove how almost unbelievably valuable the freeze, if aided by a correctly camouflaged uniform, can be, I'll tell you what I've seen on the banks of the Normanby and the

Escape rivers in Cape York Peninsula. An old dead tree, grey in one case, and brown in another, leaning out over the river-bank. I'll only refer to one tree, for precisely the same thing happened on the other river. A brown tree-snake leisurely climbed the brown tree and slithered out on to a dead branch. My mate and I had boiled the billy, leisurely keeping an eye on where the snake lay along the branch.

"He's gone," said my mate presently.

"Watch a moment," and I pointed.

"Struth!" exclaimed my mate. "Who the hell would have thought of that?"

I had seen the snake suddenly whip his tail around the branch and swiftly shoot his length up into the air on the slant, a perfect imitation of a slender, dry branch. So natural was this camouflage that my mate had said: "He's gone."

He cried, "Struth! when a bird sailing up the river had spotted that perch nicely balanced on the old, dead tree just out over the water. The bird alighted on the perch, which instantly whipped around it.

Now that snake's "uniform," and its freeze on such an utterly bare place as the bare limb of a dead tree up in the air, was so natural that it had deceived both the bird and my mate. That it deceived him was not surprising. But the bird that should have known all about such things! Think well on this true story from nature. I tell it in the hope that you will realize how supremely important camouflage and the freeze can be to you.

Maybe a morning may dawn when you are leisurely walking along and an enemy appears so suddenly there is not a second to spare in which to lie down or crouch. If so, freeze into a "statue." You may get away with it, particularly in timbered country. I have fairly good eyes, trained to the bush for thirty years past, but I've known aboriginals to stand "invisible" like that until I've ridden right up to them before seeing them. It does not always come off. Still, the less trained your enemy is, and the more unsuspecting he may be, the more often it will succeed.

The perfect stillness does it, helped by the deceptiveness of the uniform, and particularly by the way of standing. This should be as "formless" as possible. You should not look like a man. A real statue in a park is intensely conspicuous by its form; you can tell it a mile away.

Stand or crouch still as a statue but not with the form of a statue. "Hunch up" as you freeze, with hat, clothes, and limbs "blending." Be as formless as you can and you'll probably get away with it.

If you stood as a statuesque man silhouetted along a ridge, you'd be clearly and instantly visible considerably more than a mile away. But if you stood like a hunched up old stump that might be a bit of a bush, or an antbed, or any old thing, you'd get away with it.

But *remain* still until immediate danger has passed. Movement can be fatal; it generally would be. Further, while you remain still, you can see things without being seen. Many of you may at times have searched high and low for some old rogue of a horse. You're almost certain the old devil is in that little patch of scrub. He can't be, though, for you've gone through it several times. Still he has been there all the time, quietly watching you, never so much as flicking an ear or twitching his tail, let alone moving his neck, which would give a tinkle to the betraying bell. The cunning old rogue merely shuts his eyes against the irritating flies. He'll let them stay there too, so long as you're looking towards him; he won't shift them by so much as a switch of the tail. That old horse is a much larger object than a man, yet he "merges" with tree or bush or anthill and remains frozen while you walk past him with the bridle on your arm. Cultivate this freezing. Think about it. Learn all you can about it. Study the ordinary ground lark. You see it alight in a patch of grass. It disappears. You walk right up to where it must be and stand staring down at it. Yet cannot see it. It has "frozen."

Do the same if in sudden, extreme danger. If your wits are about you, you'll see or hear the enemy an instant before they see you. Freeze.

The hare freezes very effectively. Many a bird, a number of the animals, and some lizards can freeze, too. The crocodile is a huge brute of a thing. You would imagine that, in clear water, its great length and girth would be instantly discernible. Not so—not by a very long way. The crocodile, when it freezes, is one of the most difficult living things to detect. That is why again and again wild and domestic animals come to a pool to drink and practically dip their noses right into the waiting jaws.

If a twenty-foot 'gator, with its great barrel, can thus make itself invisible in water but a few yards (even feet) away, how much more invisible ought you make yourself on land—with the trees and grasses and rocks and foliage and broken earth to help hide you? Think it out. For the freeze can save your life.

CHAPTER VII
The Art of Camouflage

We come now to camouflage. If the sniper's wits can master camouflage, then truly he renders himself invisible; for an enemy may walk up to within a few feet of you, and yet not see you.

Do you realize now how strong you are? Almost invincible!

You are to be a lone fighter with an army against you. But your wits, your eyes, your ears, and the coordination of all these with the abundant help that Nature gives you makes you practically a superman. You are far superior to very many of the enemy, simply owing to your far superior knowledge of your own particular game. No armour could be invented equal to that. It renders you quite invisible. That being so, a thousand of the enemy cannot see you, cannot kill you.

Nature has saved countless billions of lives and many of her species by sending them into this ravenous world in a camouflaged coat. The grey moth, when it clings to the grey bark of tree or shrub or house beam, is invisible. It is there, its enemies are all around it. Yet while it remains still, they fail to see it

The locust, the mantis on the green of foliage or brown shrub, is invisible. You know the stick insect, how practically impossible it is to distinguish it from rosebush or shrub or bush. The green caterpillar on green foliage, the grey on grey, the brown on brown, the russet on russet, is practically invisible. The green tree-frog on the green leaves, the brown or grey or striped frog on the brown or grey bark are extraordinarily difficult to detect, even when you are looking for them. Numerous birds are "invisible" when they freeze to grass, shrub, tree, or rock of the same colour scheme as their coats. The green whipsnake is invisible so long as he lies motionless along a green bough. The tiger makes himself invisible when he freezes amongst jungle the same varying colour as his tawny, striped hide. The red 'roo is invisible when he lies at rest upon red earth below an ironstone boulder. Many a living thing is invisible so long as it clings to earth or shrub or rock bearing the same coloured coat as its own, or even different colours into which its own colouring merges. The sniper must take a lesson from this. He should become a keen student of nature in a number of things: the art of freezing, the art of camouflage, the cultivation of the senses, and intuition and instinct.

When a wild thing moves to some position where its colour scheme does not agree with the colouring, it becomes clearly visible. It must dash to cover to become invisible again, and during that dash it will be seen if an enemy is there who is seeking it. Only a few living things can remain "permanently" invisible. The chameleon is one; it can change its colour to the shade of the rock or earth upon which it rests. A species of stone-fish can do the same; it can alter its coat to the colour of the gravel or seaweed or coral upon which it rests.

The sniper is not born with that gift. But he has an

advantage in that he can use his wits to camouflage himself according to the country in which he is working.

Many parts of the Australian bush would lend themselves to dull, grey-green camouflage; the few jungle areas to slightly varying shades of green; the scrub areas to grey-green or a light, dull green according to the nature of the scrub; the ordinary forest country to greys, greens, and brownish-yellows. Our forest country varies. Yet camouflage would be easy in any of our forest lands. Because of the prevailing drab colouring, they and their earths lend themselves perfectly to camouflage.

The arid areas lend themselves to dull grey (slatey), dull khaki, or light brown according to the particular area and season. For instance, the arid spinifex (old-man spinifex as distinct from the green) of the far west is different from the arid saltbush areas of the south-west centre. "Red" country lends itself to dull red or brown; desert to a dull, yellow-tinted khaki in great areas, light brown in others; saltbush country to grey; mangrove country to dull green intersplashed with grey; and so on. These are mentioned to give you an idea of differences in country, and yet in any of these areas camouflage is quite simple.

If a sniper did not camouflage himself and his clothes to merge with the country, he would be visible to prying eyes. Remember the numerous shades and types of country in this great continent, and you begin to realize the value of studying camouflage. For instance, a man in a black shirt or flannel moving amongst grey granite boulders would be a visible target a mile away. A man in a white shirt amongst basalt would show out like a white-winged butterfly upon a brown leaf. Yet more variations occur as nature's colours change with the seasons—or through man-made activities. A ploughed field is a blanket of colour very different to the yellowish-green, dry grey, or brown grass surrounding it. A sniper invisible in the grass would immediately become visible if he crossed that ploughed area, unless he "changed his coat;" that is, camouflaged himself accordingly.

Think well upon camouflage and everything that it means. It is your cloak of invisibility. An army could not give you greater protection. If you disguise yourself in perfect camouflage and understand the freeze, with perfect confidence you can lie among the enemy and see without being seen; can ambush your man or men and never be seen; can gain priceless information and return with it; can fight and live to fight many and many other days.

By continuing to be a live and thus active sniper, you are of ever-increasing value to your countrymen and country.

You will need this camouflage when the day comes that your uniform will not completely merge with some particular area of ground upon which you wish to remain hidden, invisible. The remedy is simple. Drape a creeper over you (if creepers grow there), but arrange it naturally for all that. If lying on a patch of grass, arrange tufts of grass upon back and cap or hat, in your belt, and upon chest and legs, too, if you must move about. Do the job as naturally as possible, for an enemy may appear only a few yards away, and if he's a sniper himself and suspicious, then his eyes and wits will be sharp—he will be looking for you. If you've clumsily arranged grass over you with the roots showing, his eyes may be attracted to those roots and he'll instantly "take a tumble," for grass roots do not grow above ground.

It is surprising the number of otherwise canny men of every nation under the sun who overlook such vital details. I knew a Turkish sniper once who lost his life all because of a handful of red poppies. He was a crafty sniper, too, as was proved by the twenty-six identity disks strung around his neck. Goodness knows how many other men he'd killed whose disks he could not souvenir. He was neatly camouflaged in a green field bright with patches of red poppies. His field grey uniform was blended perfectly with the green barley he had draped upon it, his loose, crinkled cap was naturally camouflaged, as were his legs—and particularly his feet. He had even twisted barley around his forehead and cheek bones. His rifle too was painted green. To add the perfect touch, he had pulled a handful of poppies and draped them across his back. He'd been too confidently lazy to finalize this last touch, for one poppy was lying upside down. Then he had gone to sleep.

Nothing was doing anyway. In the far distance there was the occasional faint "pop-pop-pop" of rifle shots as some patrol engaged an outpost in a little private war of its own. Otherwise there was no sign of any enemy. The sun was nice and warm. It can be very drowsy in a barley-field on a morning such as that. Slowly the Turkish sniper's head drooped upon his hands; his cheek nestled down as he drowsed into his last sleep.

It was a wandering patrol that did it, the horses' hooves being muffled in the soft earth. The sergeant halted; he'd gone far enough, and there was no sign of the enemy. He decided to dismount for a smoke-oh before turning back. One of the troopers, a lad and an amateur soldier at that, wandered aside for a moment. He almost sat down on a poppy that was growing upside down. Curiously he looked at it—then suddenly his mouth opened to yell. He stopped in the nick of time, thrust down his rifle, and fired.

CHAPTER VIII
Invisibility Is Salvation

A man cannot, of course, always be exact in detail. For instance, when he stands up, his camouflage would vary in position. But it was one tiny oversight in detail that cost the sniper in the last chapter his life. He could have slept on and the lad would have been unaware of his presence had it not been for that upside-down poppy.

Detail does not matter nearly so much at a distance, of course. But when the invader lands, much of the fighting will be at close quarters. Detail in personal camouflage will then matter a great deal; at very close quarters it will become a matter of life and death

Fate may bring you on to clayey ground. If so, smear yourself with clay; if on muddy country, use mud; if on dusty, use dust. At any time when on business, "use" the country; become part of the earth upon which you walk or lie or hide; make yourself invisible with leaves, or earth stains, or with lightly teased strips of bark, with the broad leaves of the jungle or the grass of the forest, with the rushes of the stream or the spinifex of the desert, with the wheat of the field or the seaweed of the seashore, with the lawyer-leaved palm of the tropics or the saltbush of the arid lands, with the charcoal of night or the ochres of the coloured lands, with the bracken of the creeks, or with tea-tree bark to make you grey as the granite rocks. Use your wits and eyes to make you one with the very earth upon which you walk or hide. Nature places the very materials at hand, no matter where you may be.

It is the invisible sniper who lives the longest, who does by far the greater damage to the enemy. Remember, you will be up against not only specially trained but desperate men, as well. They know we will fight craftily and desperately. They will land on a foreign shore, far from home, and their one objective will be to advance and kill quickly, and kill again. The enemy will realize that there will be no hope for him if his comrades are beaten. Furthermore, he is that most dangerous of fighters, the fanatic. Hence, every one of these men will be on the lookout for you! Thus you cannot afford to throw a single chance away.

Remember, too, that you are now looked up to as a highly specialized man. When you volunteer to be a sniper, you practically offer to throw your life away—at a heavy price. Your object is to hold your life to the very last in order to kill as many as you can and thus save the lives of many of your comrades. Each deadly shot you fire means an enemy less to take the life of a comrade. Prove worthy of the respect and trust your soldier and civilian comrades repose in you.

Prove yourself worthy of being looked up to as a sniper. Always remember your face and hands, then your boots. It is these that show up the plainest at close quarters, and the attraction to prying eyes of light reflected from them will give the show away. An aeroplane can pass over a squadron of men without seeing them, so long as they merge with the earth and lie or squat motionless. But let only one man look up and the sunlight reflect from his face, and then bombs and streams of machine-gun bullets will promptly be the result. They may not get the man who looked up, but some will get his mates.

As a rule you will be fighting alone. If you allow your face to betray you, you will get it in the neck—and it serves you right.

Use your common sense in camouflage. Do not overdo it. Remember that nature is almost always "natural." Though the human eye misses countless natural things, it immediately is attracted to anything unnatural. And so is human curiosity. If your camouflage is unnatural, an unfriendly eye will examine it with quick curiosity.

If you saw a dog in the distance, you'd probably take no notice. It would apparently be a dog. But if that dog appeared to grow a tuft of feathers instead of hair, you'd immediately investigate.

Therefore be certain your camouflage is natural.

Although nature has millions of differing landscapes, they always seem to "fit in." Your camouflage must fit in. Although nature grows countless billions of tufts of grass, every single tuft seems to fit in. So don't "grow" your grass or leaves or ochre in the wrong place. Don't "grow" a huge tuft of grass on your head or shoulders if the grass around you is scanty. If you are hiding in a paddock where the grass is yellowing under summer, do not camouflage yourself with a green bush, because a noticeable green in a landscape of yellow catches the eye immediately.

That the unusual in nature attracts the eye seems to be a rule of nature. A distant peak, a bluff, or a lake immediately attracts the eye. At close quarters, unusual little things similarly attract the eye.

One distinct colour different from all near it is visible

from a great distance. Many a time I've stood on a precipice in the north Queensland jungle country and gazed out over a sea of foliage. Immediately the scarlet of a flame-tree caught my eye across the gorge a mile away. Then another tree, all white flowers. The eye would wander unseeing over miles of jungle green only to come to attention at one speck of yellow foliage half a mile away.

So make sure that there is nothing unusual about your camouflage to put you away.

In these warfare days of infiltration tactics, you probably quite often will find yourself behind the enemy lines. Again and again you may have to lie doggo while a strong band of the enemy passes by.

Then you start shooting again, constantly using your head while waging your own little war.

Under these and other circumstances, if you have not made yourself invisible, you stand grave risks of being seen. Bands of the enemy may pass by within a few yards. You could kill two or three, perhaps more, but you would be killed. Your value would then be gone. Your job is to last out as long as you possibly can. So stain your face and hands and break up the colouring. By using your wits, you probably would account for half a dozen that day, half a dozen the next, and so on. Camouflage your footwear and hat or cap. You would not be fool enough to be wearing anything white, or any metal thing which glints. Even one shiny metal button or bright piece of tin or piece of glass can reflect light miles away. These things sound simple, but don't lose your life to a simple thing. Your own empty shell case could put you away on a bright day. The cartridge case is brass, which could give a glint from the sun. Eject each shell carefully and slip it under you or anywhere away from a chance ray of the sun. Take no chances in this game.

So far as your uniform and clothes are concerned, these may depend on the army authorities. If you are in the regulars, your uniform will probably be khaki. The dull Australian khaki is a good hiding material providing one lies quite still, but it is much more noticeable than is generally supposed if one is moving. A mixture of grey and green with dashes of a yellowish tinge, especially if irregularly shaped splotches of dull "bark" white are added, would merge well with most of our Australian landscape. However, if in the regulars and sent away out from the lines, camouflage your uniform to the best possible advantage. If in the irregulars, you'll have more opportunity for doing this. No matter in what particular arm of our defenders you may be, don't forget that I'm going to write a little later on about your shape. That is considerably more important even than camouflage.

Whatever your uniform, don't wear shiny or glossy material. You will be under bright sunlight many a day, sometimes bright moonlight at night. Always remember that any glossy material reflects light, and light instantly catches the eye. Naturally so, for it is by reflected light that the eye sees objects.

Remember then that any shiny metallic object reflects light that can be seen even miles away, and that a glossy object, even cloth, reflects light that may be caught by the eye an appreciable distance away. But a dull, indistinct material barely reflects at all; it scatters in all directions any light that touches it. Hence the light is swallowed up in the surroundings. Absorb these facts and you will realize how important is the material in your uniform.

If, unavoidably, you are sent out someday in clothes of a shiny material, rub them over with dust. Better dirty clothes than a bullet through the ribs.

In the last war, snipers' suits were made to make a man

practically invisible, so long as he "froze" to the ground, even at a distance of only two feet. We seem to have forgotten some of the worthwhile lessons of the last war.

If your clothes are carefully thought-out, you can bring yourself very close to invisibility by adding natural camouflage, by using whatever offers in the country upon which you are operating, and by cautiously draping or smearing yourself with the materials which in every locality nature lays open to you.

Learn something else. A keen eye may be gazing down upon your country from a height. If you wear uniform alone, and if that uniform is considerably lighter, or much darker, than the earth upon which you are lying, quite possibly you will be spotted. Even if the uniform were the same *colour* as the surroundings, its distinctly lighter or darker shade could attract a searching eye from a height. If you are operating on open country at a lower level than some of the surrounding country, always remember that an enemy on a crag above may be searching the lower country through powerful glasses. He thus has an advantage, magnified considerably should you incautiously move.

So not only brightness in clothes, but the shades themselves, can count. No matter at what level of country you may be operating in, you must be so arrayed that actually you and every part of you "melt" into the earth and surroundings. Accomplish that and you will live a long time. An enemy can then pass within two feet of you and not see you. He can search for you at any angle with glasses and not detect you. You will have made yourself invisible.

CHAPTER IX
Form and Formlessness

Nature loves colour. She flaunts it for all to see. The human eye loves colour, and catches it. The feminine sex instinctively realize this secret. Your face is colour. It is almost unbelievable the distance at which the eye will pick out just a speck of colour. So, when on dangerous work, give particular attention to your ugly face. You may be proud of it, but it may unwittingly betray you.

Here is a secret. Although colour is visible from afar, if you "break it up," it merges into the background, becomes drab like the background. Hence if you stained your face or rubbed a bit of ochre or a smear or two of charcoal over it, that breaks up the white splotch. But don't use the one colour all over the face (unless black at nighttime). Rub a bit of brown, or better still grey dust, or a splash of other colour over it to "break it up." If you painted your face yellow all over, for instance, it would still be a splash of colour.

Your face may seem a small thing, easy to hide. It is and it isn't. For you, a sniper, it is a matter of vital importance.

And so are your arms and hands. Hide your brawny arms—brawn will not stop a bullet but it will attract one. If you are used to shooting with your sleeves rolled up, take my advice and work in long sleeves when sniping. An enemy half a mile or more away may have a glass. And he'll easily pick out your arms.

To bring straight into your mind how really important such things as freeze, cover, and camouflage are to you, I'll show you a little picture, a picture that surely all of you have seen. And yet, only one in a hundred of you have seen it, for neither your wits nor your eyes have been trained to see. While seeing, you have been blind.

This picture is of a bushie chopping down a tree. You were walking or riding along. You hear the ring of an axe. Your ears correctly tell you that someone is swinging an axe. Presently you see the bushman, for your ears take your eyes to him down there by the creek. You watch him a while, for every one is interested, unfortunately, in seeing a tree chopped down. Presently you pass on. You have seen everything.

But have you? We will see. The tree is a drab old warrior of the bush. The bushie looks drab too. He wears a crinkled, drab old slouch hat; his shirt sleeves are rolled up; he wears a waistcoat, unbuttoned; his loosely fitting pants crinkled out of shape have seen a lot of work; his big boots are crinkled too.

Suddenly you realize that the bushie's clothes are as drab as the gnarled old trunk of the tree. If he stood still against it you would hardly see him.

Wait. He swings the axe again. Instantly you see his strong, bare arm. That arm alone would reveal him half a mile away. It stands out startlingly distinct each time he swings the axe. Then you see the flash of the blade, then the gleam of the polished handle. Even if the axe made no sound, the flash of the blade would put the man away. You have hardly seen his face, but now you see one cheek plainly each time he swings back the axe. You notice something else, his shirt sleeve; it is lighter than his drab clothes. Swiftly then your eye fastens to the line of shirt that shows between waist-coat and belt each time the axeman swings the axe. If he were wearing a grey or black flannel, your eyes would never have been attracted to these parts of the man, for they would have merged with his clothes and the tree.

The next thing you notice is the scar in the tree. It comes as a bit of a shock to realize you would never even have noticed the tree but for the bright gap in it cut by the axe. Then you notice the chips, for upon their light colour the sun is reflecting. There is nothing drab about that fresh gap in the tree, those fresh chips. How plainly they stand out! That is because their fresh colouring does not merge with the drab outer colouring of the tree. Realize now what simple things have attracted you to that man chopping the tree. Forget the sound of the axe. It is these little things that have attracted your eye to him: first, his bare, brown forearm; next, the glint of the axe blade; next, his cheek under his hat; then the momentary gleam of light on the axe handle; next, the sleeve of the shirt and the little piece exposed between waistcoat and belt. All else is quite indistinct.

If that man had worn a long-sleeved, dark flannel, if his face and arms had been stained, and if he had frozen against that tree, then you would have passed within feet of him and not seen him.

So now you realize, apart from sound, how a few simple things can betray a full-grown man chopping at a huge tree. Realize then how a very simple thing, one solitary little thing, could betray you, a sniper, to a keen, questing eye.

There is something else you presently learn, something deeper than colour, something even more important than camouflage. That crinkled old hat. You've hardly noticed he had a hat. At a little distance it seems to merge into the surroundings. You stare puzzled as this strange fact penetrates your consciousness. The hat helps to hide the head, and it merges into the surroundings—because it has no *form*. If the bushie wore a well-shaped hat like yours, one would see it instantly. Also the features under it.

The man himself does not seem to stand out, from the hat right down. That shapeless old waistcoat opens all the way to allow his arms full movement. How wonderfully it camouflages the upper body, seems to do away with its shape, exactly as the hat does the head.

Then the trousers. They are drab, loose, built for comfort in working. They quite disguise the form of the lower half of the body. And the feet. You simply do not notice them, for the loose trouser-leg bottoms "fall" over the big, crinkled, unshapely boots.

Suddenly you realize how differently this man would look, how his form would stand out, if he wore a well-fitting suit of clothes. You would see him a mile away.

But none of his clothes have form. And this causes him to lose form himself. Shapelessness is extremely important; it is more important even than camouflage.

If you have no form, you do not appear to be a man. And it is men which the enemy are seeking to shoot.

You perhaps have noticed, for instance, how a curlew "frozen" to earth is almost invisible, or a brown frog against a brown tree-trunk, or the old mopoke squatting upon the stump, almost invisible; you think Nature has achieved a masterpiece there, that she's unbeatable. She is not. You can outdo her. When by accident you've spotted the mopoke and walk up to and stare at and touch it to make sure it really is a bird, what is it that has put him away? You cannot tell. His colouring perfectly merges with the stump, while his body appears actually a part of it. He is motionless as a dead thing. What then is it that has really betrayed him?

It is his shape (form). Everything—animal, bird, man— has a shape, a body, and thus forms a distinct and recognizable outline. And the eye instinctively looks for that outline You can outdo nature even by camouflaging your shape. This is very important indeed.

You alter your outline as much as is humanly possible and not only merge into earth and background, but "melt" into it. Thus, the outline vanishes. Apart from clothes or camouflage, you no longer look like a man. And the eye does not recognize you.

This can only be done by more or less baggy clothes and the attitude of the body when freezing. Any fairly tight-fitting clothes make outline—shape. Get well into your mind this shape, this form. It is you! Disguise it, and you are set.

Do you realize what puts an object away? It is form, shadow, and reflection of light.

Take any bird you wish that is perfectly camouflaged when squatting down. When it stands up you can see it. When it squats, you cannot, or hardly.

When it stands it has both shadow and form; it can disguise neither. It may or may not merge with its surroundings so far as cover and camouflage are concerned, but it cannot disguise its shape and shadow. Its shape is the outline of a bird to which by some mysterious way the eye is drawn, helped by the shadow. But when the bird squats, it flattens out, becoming a shred of bark, a tuft of grass, a clod of earth, a chip from the tree, or a shadow among all the countless shadows of the grassy world. In short, it is a thing without form.

Realize that fact. Camouflage yourself, but first make yourself a thing without form and you can defy detection by an army.

The only way to make yourself without form is to have no distinct shape about you. No distinct shape or outline of cap or hat, of tunic or pants or boots. Then when you lie down or freeze against rock or tree, you melt into the very earth, become part of the very rock, part of the very tree.

You become invisible.

Remember your ears. They were made to hear with. But, like your eyes, they will not hear so that *you* can hear unless *you* ask. Train them to do so.

How many sounds do you hear in a day? Very few indeed. Thousands of sounds certainly impinge on your ears, but you register only half a dozen of them. That is because you are not interested. You will hear the dinner bell; you'll hear the knock-off whistle; you'll hear the baby howling; you'll hear conversation addressed to you, and a few other sounds in the meaning of which you are interested. All the rest are null and void.

This is quite all right in ordinary life, but not in *your* life. You are going to be a sniper, and the sounds that will be there for you to hear will be very different indeed. Hence, train concentration on your hearing so that the ears grow instinctively to be always listening, always ready instantly to register.

The soft thud of a horse's hoof on soft soil should come as an immediate warning to freeze. But your ear will never hear it, never register the sound and meaning, unless you train it. Your ears should be set to be constantly "thinking" of the direction of the wind, of the slightest breeze, of the unfelt wind currents. For it is on these currents that sound carries more swiftly. If your ears are not attuned to their direction, they may easily miss a soft sound. They should catch a murmured conversation in a deep trench nearby, or a whispering in the grass; the crack of a twig under a stealthy foot, or the rustle in the grass that is an enemy creeping on his belly.

It is not so much the big sounds they should hear but the little sounds that warn of stealthy danger nearby. The incautious striking of a match has been known to betray a man by the sound alone. Countless men have been betrayed through careless walking, the crunch of their boots on gravel, the swish of long grass, the kicking of a stone, the splash when stamping through water, the tinkle of a food utensil, or the thud of a rifle butt against ground, tree, or rock. There are countless "little sounds" which can be big with meaning for you. Train your ears to be ever-seeking to hear things. Then you will be surprised at the things you will hear. Surprised too and interested to realize that your ears are beginning to "listen in" with your eyes, just as your eyes learn to "see in" with your wits.

For these organs of your body, these allies of yours, by acute training, not only develop extraordinarily, they actually begin to "work in" with one another. Encourage them all you can, for it means your life.

One day you will be in hostile country. Cautiously you gaze around. Nothing out of the ordinary is visible, but your trained wits are seeking something. Although you see absolutely nothing but the landscape, those wits are extraordinarily suspicious; they are seeking something all the time. And the eyes are working in with them, trying hard to see the "something" the wits suspect may be there. Presently the eyes rest on a clump of timber, maybe a bunch of bracken, or just an old log with grass growing around it. There's nothing there. But again and again the eyes come back to that spot. Still, there's nothing there. The ears are seeking any faint sound that may come on a vagrant air current, analysing any sound that comes so as to help the eyes and suspicious wits. Suddenly the ears catch the faintest cough, and instantly the eyes switch to that bracken. The wits now know there is an enemy concealed there.

It was the ears that actually "saw" that enemy, the trained ears working in conjunction with eyes and wits. Otherwise the wits would not have known, the eyes could not have seen; perhaps the enemy is so well hidden that they do not see him even now. But wits, eyes, and ears now know he is there.

It is imperative to train the ears so. They can actually see for you when the eyes fail to locate a danger.

Don't forget the nose. Seek to train this, too, and it also will become a willing, eager ally working in with the wits and eyes and ears. What, under various circumstances, these fail to detect, the nose may. The faint whiff of smoke from a hidden fire, the sweat from a horse, a whiff from food being cooked, a whiff of gasolene, a whiff of tobacco smoke, a smell of nearby man.

For humans have their distinctive odour just as an animal has. Just ask the older abo what our smell is like and he will turn up his nose in disgust. At the same time the abo, though he might deny it, packs a smell that is a real humdinger. All coloured and Asiatic people can distinctly smell *our* smell, and we can detect theirs. So that there is more in your nose than you wot of. But you must urge the nasal appendage to cultivate its smells.

You realize now how many close natural friends you have, and how very many natural allies you have in nature. Cultivate your close personal friends, get to know them, and they will know and serve you. Take every advantage you can of all that nature constantly offers you, and no longer will you feel alone. As you realize what strong aids your wits and eyes are, and how you can make yourself "invisible," you will grow in confidence until you'll delight to go out alone; delight to infiltrate behind the enemy, to get right in amongst them and play merry hell—and get yourself safely out again.

CHAPTER X
Preparing for Action

We will imagine now that you are on the warpath. Out after scalps.

From the moment you leave battalion or camp, your life is in your own hands.

The enemy have landed on the coast; advance bands of them are attempting to filter in

Distantly you hear the boom of guns. But that battle is not your battle. Two enemy scouting planes appear over the hilltops, coming swiftly on, soon directly overhead. You crouch down, not looking up. You are only one lone man, and the keen-eyed observers above, even with their powerful glasses, should not see you. You walk cautiously on.

The main body of the enemy is held up a good many miles away. But they have sent out bodies of men far to the flanks. These bodies again have split up into smaller parties, cautiously attempting to slip past our troops. These smaller parties have again split up into groups of from three to five. At wide intervals, these trained men are slipping on ahead through the bush.

A bush unknown to them. Whereas you know the bush. Even though not a local bushman, you possess a far, far better knowledge of the Australian country than the invader.

And this knowledge is going to prove of great value. When a burglar breaks into a man's house, the householder, if awake, holds an invincible advantage. So it is with you.

You are making towards a quiet road that winds among the hills several miles away. You have reasoned it out this way: the main body of the enemy is held up on the coast. Their advance parties will try and infiltrate southwest, for that direction offers the easiest way through these hills. Also, a southwesterly direction will take them quickest through the hills, then out on to open country into which their main body can pour their mechanized units. So the enemy infiltrators will seek to learn the quickest and easiest way for their main body. Soon after leaving the coast, some of their advanced scouts must cut that road. They will naturally follow it down, for it will be the easiest and quickest way and surest guide to their objective, the country inland. I'll pick a good possy commanding some favourable portion of that road and get set for a little steady shooting.

By reasoning thus, you know where to go straight to a target; no time is wasted. And you will be going to a position where there will be shooting and where you may gain information of extreme importance to the military command defending this particular area of the coastline.

As you walk, you keep down in among the hills, around the ends of spurs as much as possible, naturally avoiding the skyline. But you walk bush in such a way that you constantly see the skyline on the hills and ridges ahead, and as far as possible to your right or left, according to the direction from which you are advancing.

Thus you are constantly under cover but at the same time will first see any enemy who may come popping up over the ridges within view.

You know you have ample time. But you know also that the unexpected often happens in warfare, particularly in this war. Thus your wits must be working constantly to guard you against surprise.

You reach the road edge. There is no need to walk right out on to it; that would be foolish anyway, for you might leave betraying tracks. Examine that road; it holds the latest and most truthful war information for you. Are there enemy tracks upon it? Those tracks will be going down the road, southwest. Are there tracks of motorcyclists, cars, tanks, cavalrymen, or infantry? No, the dust is undisturbed. But make sure. Choose some hard part of the road where you yourself will leave no tracks. Cross the road to that cutting opposite. Make sure there are no solitary tracks of enemy scouts—of infiltrators.

None. Good. You have got there first as you anticipated. Now, cross back again, for it is there the hills are highest, and on that side, for various geographical reasons, will be your best and safest possy.

Now comes the most important thing of all: selecting your position.

The dull, brown road winds between hills. There are a thousand possible possies on either side of the road.

But every one of those good possies might mean a death-trap for you. You'd shoot a few men—but you'd never live to shoot another day.

On high country (but not crossing any skyline) you walk along, carefully examining the contour of the road. Finally you come to a bend, a long, boomerang-shaped bend. The "arm" towards the coast appears in plain view for more than a mile before it vanishes among the hills. The arm leading inland runs for half a mile in plain view between slightly higher hills. The elbow upon which you are standing is a big hill, lightly timbered, with plenty of natural cover. Not only does this larger hill command the complete bend from right to left, it commands the country directly opposite. The hills there, just across the road, are much lower, and with much less cover on them. Many of their slopes fall gently, and are covered only by short grass and an occasional tree and rock.

You can see right over these hills and, except for inevitable patches of dead ground, out across the little flats and lower hills behind and on either side of them. You glance along the country to your right and can see in among those hills also, for your hill commands them, too.

You now have a wonderful position. Your elbow commands the road to right and left; no matter where an enemy may appear along two miles of that road, he will come under your rifle sights. And he cannot cross that road without your seeing him. Your elbow also looks down upon the hills directly opposite, so that an enemy leaving the road to tackle you from the front will be within easy range and visible. If he tries an outflanking movement from the right you will see it, and again and again must see him as he creeps closer. You can pot at him as he comes down the road or attempts to outflank you from the hills to the right, or to attack you from the hills to the front, or to outflank you away to your left front. Not only will he be under your rifle fire, his numbers and movements will again and again become visible to you.

The country directly behind you and veering back from your left is your getaway, the country along which you have come. From this position you will see any enemy advance at least a mile away; and when they come close, you can stay here and overlook their movements over all the country in a semicircle from your right around your front to your extreme left flank. You can snipe from this position for quite a long time—until they have three parts surrounded you. And at the last moment you will be able to get away with the greatest of ease.

From this position you can kill but not be killed. A sniper should always try to do that, unless ordered to hold some post to the last.

All that remains now is to pick your actual firing possy and to camouflage yourself as may be necessary. Pick the firing position which will give you in greatest detail all the advantages enumerated. This particular hill offers you all those advantages. But you must pick the ideal spot upon it which offers you every advantage in greatest detail, with the greatest personal cover and the easiest access to a quiet getaway.

That should be fairly simple. Your hill commands the others and is higher than they. Unless you are an utter goat, you will pick a commanding possy from which the enemy will not see any of you to fire at. They will crawl up the nearby hills trying to locate you. But you will be higher; you will be firing down and they will be firing up. Should they imagine they see anything to fire at, or simply open fire in an attempt to draw your fire and thus locate you, there should be none of you exposed to either their sight or bullet.

Having selected your possy, what about the earth immediately under your rifle barrel? If dry and powdery it will betray you. For the blast from the rifle muzzle will blow up a little puff of dust. That is what experienced soldiers look for. The sound, of course, is a guide, but it is the puff of smoke or dust that puts the position away. If the earth is so dry and powdery that the dust mixes with the smokey gases from the rifle muzzle, then the position may be immediately betrayed.

The enemy will know exactly where you are. They will put a machine gun onto you; without further loss of time they will split up to circle around and "get" you, leaving a man or two in front to keep you occupied. You would have had every opportunity but would have failed as a real sniper. Your only chance now would be to slip swiftly away.

But, if you were not in such a tactical possy as described, you would not see them starting out to work around you. In that case, if you were unaware that your rifle blast has put you away, you would stay in the possy until you get a bayonet or bullet in the back.

Be sure then that the earth under your rifle muzzle cannot put you away. If the muzzle is firing out into space, the blast will raise no wisp of dust, but if too much of the barrel is exposed it might be noticed. Also, you must consider the puff of vapour from the exploded gases.

If firing out over moist ground, green grass, or a hard rock surface upon which there was *no sign of fine dust*, you would be set. There are scores of conditions under which you can fire a rifle with no chance of the muzzle blast putting you away. Now you know of the danger from a dusty or powdery earth surface and you can guard against it.

The next thing to guard against is the puff of smoky vapour from the gases which spurt from the muzzle on explosion. Smokeless cartridges are not yet perfected.

Certain conditions of atmosphere and the position of the sun, allied to contour and height from which you are firing, tend to make this puff of vapour noticeable.

If you could, while clinging to an unobstructed view, do your shooting so that vapour was "taken up" by bushes or among rocks or trees, then the vapour would not be seen. Your camouflaged self and your position would be absolutely invisible.

Make your position as comfortable as possible. You may have to sit or lie in it for hours. You will observe much more clearly and shoot much more accurately if you are comfortable.

The next thing to consider is your front. Your actual front at the start will not be the hill or hills directly opposite across the road but the extreme visible end of the road away to the right. It is down there that the enemy will almost certainly first appear.

Survey and endeavour to memorize the country away up there. Then estimate distance most carefully, the distance at which you believe the enemy will first come into sight. You are now finding the ranges on this, your coming battlefield. Every shot, when the time comes, must find a mark. If you cannot estimate distances, then your shooting will deteriorate accordingly. Every shot which has an enemy means one less of them to hunt you down.

Your eyes wander up along the road, resting on outstanding landmarks to the right and left. There's a rock with a plain white splash across it, just by the left of the track—about 1,000 yards. Very carefully you confirm this, to the best of your judgment. (Range estimation was discussed in *Shoot to Kill*, so we won't go over the ground again.) At a glance anytime throughout the day, you will instantly be able to "pick up" the rock; it will be a base for your range, just 1,000 yards. To there, and to right and left of it across both sides of the road, you have the range. From that rock (or whatever landmark it may be) you estimate back down the road towards you—700 yards, 600, 500. Ah! Just about exactly halfway between you and the 1,000-yard range stands a splintered tree once struck by lightning. Your eyes can pick it up at any second under any circumstances.

You now have your 500-yard range, an important range.

From that point, a hundred yards nearer you is a landslide with the red clay showing vividly. This is the 400-yard range. And that big stump which has rolled down from the cutting is the 300 yards. And now you have the range all along that most important bend of the road to the right. Similarly, you "mark" the ranges to your immediate front. And then down the road to the left.

You feel you have done a really good job. They haven't appeared yet. You feel quite comfortable and confident. You hear the dull boom of guns. "Sounds a bit closer," you think. "I wonder how the boys are faring." And instantly you turn to planning your own battle.

"Let me see now. They'll come straight down the road. A shot or two and they'll scatter to the hills, almost certainly to the left, for the shots will be coming from this direction and the left side of the road from me will offer them the quickest and apparently safest cover."

Thus you try to foresee just what will happen. The country is spread out before you to help you judge. You put yourself in the place of the enemy leader coming down the road. What will he do when you open fire? You answer it by knowing what you would do were you in his place. Then you plan ahead again, a move ahead of him all the time.

Having decided what he probably will do when you open fire, you think: "Now, instead of blazing at them when they appear up the road, could I get more of them by letting them get a lot closer?" Cunningly, you study the road even more closely, and the country to either side. Finally you notice this:

On the right-hand side of the road, just opposite the shattered tree, the hills are abruptly steep, difficult for men in a great hurry to climb. But to the left is a break between the hills, and the hills themselves are merely gentle rises. From your position you can see all over those hills, around the back of them, and around the sides of them.

A startled enemy would jump to the left (his right) in a dash, for that easy cover. At a glance he would see he could reach cover there quicker than on the opposite side of the road. But you would still see him. He wouldn't be aware of it, but as his men scattered, the hiding place that most of them sought would be in plain view to you away up here on your eyrie. Hence, by waiting for advancing enemy to come right down the road to this spot, you would not only get a clear and much closer shot at one and perhaps two of them while they were still on the road, but you would also be able to continue shooting at them while they were under "cover."

You grin; decide you're a bit of a general—or a corporal at least. Such a pleasing discovery has increased your fire power by at least 50 percent. Instead of now being certain of any one clear shot at one man at 1,000 yards, you should now get five clear shots at five men. Perhaps more.

You get busy at working out what the enemy will do after your shots have thinned him down a little and he finally gets into cover. Your right flank should be safe, providing he makes that obvious dash to his right, which of course is your left. But if any of the enemy do dash to the other side of the road, you must see them and can act accordingly. Such a move would make your position less tenable as time went on, but at least you would know that the danger was there and would gradually be working towards you. But they almost certainly will do as you thought, principally because the lay of the country lends itself to that very action.

You still plan it out. After the first shots and the scatter, the enemy now will try desperately hard to get you. The surprise has been complete; as yet he has but a very vague idea of where you are. He is in a strange country, and again and again you will see him.

In short rushes he will carry on trying to get around your front wherever he may conclude it may be; he will try to shoot you from there, or to get around you. Your eyes sweep away to the left, your left bend in the road. Unless he dashes down the road by armoured car, of course, it will take him a long time to work around there. You will have done a lot of damage by then. And when he finally does cross the road away down there, you will see him and know just when to make an easy getaway, or a getaway back to another position where *you* can outflank *his* flankers.

Providing there are not too many of him, and under some quick-witted leader, you may be able to carry on the battle until nightfall. Again you think what a fine general you'd make. You feel absolutely confident; you wish he'd come. Your eye wanders back up along to the extreme end of the road—and the old ticker suddenly misses a beat. Three black dots are showing up above the skyline. So they are not coming down the road after all!

You get the glasses onto them. Yes, they are the enemy right enough. Using glasses too. You now feel very glad that you understand your game, that you have made yourself into a trained sniper and that now you are "invisible."

With a thrill of confidence you carefully train the glasses down along that distant ridge, examining every tuft of rock on the skyline, every stone, every tree. You *must* know, if at all possible, the number of enemy there.

You can see only three. Immediately, you try to guess what the enemy noncommissioned officer will do. First, does he know his job? Is he keeping other men hidden behind that ridge? If he sends any to cross the road, you will see them; if he advances you will see him and the men with him. You must watch not only his movements but the road too, lest he cunningly outflank you. He won't attempt to do that until he learns that you are there. Through his glasses he is examining the road very closely and the hills to either side. He is suspicious of that bend.

Distantly, you hear the boom of guns.

CHAPTER XI
The Sniper Fights

One black dot vanishes. Instantly you are alert for any movement by any of the enemy, for every movement is of vital importance to you. What you miss may mean your death.

Why has he vanished? To move to a position where you now fail to locate him? To give an order to men unseen? To signal a larger body of men behind? That probably is it. You have seen enemy planes fly low down over that road. They must have reported back the location of the road and that it apparently is unoccupied by us.

Enemy headquarters has passed the word on to these advance infiltrators, and here they are. Their job is to find out whether we hold the road.

No sooner thought than you glance away back up the road. It is bare; even the glasses show no signs of life where the road vanishes amongst distant hills. You glance to the ridge again. Ah! He is back. The three heads are there. Whatever he wanted to do, he has done.

What did he want to do? Keenly alert, you watch both ridge and the distant end of the road.

Ah! Here they come. The tiny figures of men appear away up the road. You turn the glasses on them. Two—five—eight—ten—fifteen—twenty—twenty-five. Twenty-five men, spread out across the road at intervals of ten yards between each man back along the road. They don't intend to become a ready-made target for a machine-gun burst. Confidently but at the ready, they come marching along.

So that was it. He had climbed down from the skyline to signal a larger body of men that the road appeared clear to the bend at least. And now, a little farther along the ridge, appear two more heads. So he had two men in reserve. You are glad he did not send them across the road to work down among the hills to that big hill which commands the bend your hill. You reckon you could easily have got both men had that scout leader done so. But you would have missed what promises to be a fine lot of shooting.

You chuckle quietly. Your present possy seems so perfectly obvious now, the perfect position both for friend or foe. You could easily have taken any one of those other thousand positions along the road. But any one of them would have commanded the road—for a shot or two *only*.

You are thankful now that you have worked incessantly to train your wits. You know well why the scout leader came the way he did, why he halted, why he did not send those other two men to cross the road. It is because the very things he did have been the safest and surest for him; he had advanced and acted naturally, according to the lie of the country. By the way he has advanced, he has been able to see clearly any low hills that line that side of the road, and see the road too. Coming the way he has done, he can gain his information by the quickest way while taking the least chance of walking into an ambush. And if he is attacked, he can fight or retire as he pleases.

These considerations you thought out for yourself, and they helped in the decision to occupy your present possy.

The twenty-five men are now in plain view, coming down the road. What now?

An enemy reconnaissance plane appears behind the men and roars on low down over the road. You see pilot and observer as they peer down; then they have vanished down the bend. In minutes only they come back and you see a message fluttering down. They have advised the patrol that from the air they see no sign of enemy.

Your face sets grim. The enemy must be anxious to prove quickly this road. If that patrol can reach the open country unobstructed, they will wireless or signal the plane, which will advise headquarters that the road is clear of enemy. And then—the first mechanized troops will come pouring down

You are only one man. Suddenly you realize that this road, this elbow of the road, may well prove of vital importance to the whole Australian Army. Your teeth clench; you have decided not only to carry out what before would have been your easy duty as a sniper, but now to hold the enemy back from obtaining their vital information to the very last. To gain time for that army fighting hard where that growing boom of the guns is coming. The twenty-five enemy have now reached the 1,000-yard mark, that white splashed rock. They are coming on quickly since they received that aeroplane message that the road, apparently, is clear. The five men on the ridge away behind but to their right stay there; you realize they are a covering party in case the men going down the road are attacked.

When those advancing men safely reach the bend, you know that the five behind will then come quickly after them.

Your brain is clear as crystal. Despite the aeroplane message, you feel sure the patrol leader will not chance leading his men into a possible ambush; he will split them up. He will send half a dozen down the road to the bend. Once there they will climb the big hill—*your* hill. From there they will obtain a clear view of the hidden portion of the bend and of the country to either side, and then signal their leader that all is clear.

Meanwhile, the officer with the remainder of his men will cover their advance, from—where?

Instantly you know: from where they nearly are now, from the splintered tree, the 500-yard range. The officer will see the opening and the vantage point of the low hills so easily of accessible from the roadside. From there he can cover the advance or retreat of his men until they reach the very summit of that big hill that commands the bend.

They are almost there—almost by the splintered tree. You have used your wits, have forestalled their every move except one. You know now that the officer will group his men together near the splintered tree.

Slowly you settle the rifle to your shoulder. You already have picked out the officer.

He pauses. A move of his hand and his soldiers verge in towards him. They group as he orders a noncom to go down the road to the bend and climb that big hill. Along your rifle sights you see him pointing directly towards you. Your sights are at his belt buckle, steadily you raise the sights six inches higher up on him. "Crack!" As he crumples up you've whipped back the bolt and reloaded and have the sights on the startled enemy crouching around the fallen officer. "Crack!" You've got another man as they bound up and race for cover, the easiest cover to reach, that gap between the low rises to the left of the road. They are breaking a marathon as they race that hundred yards. You are following a man steadily, with your rifle sighted a few feet ahead of him. Carefully you are estimating his speed; then just before he reaches cover, "Crack!—and he plunges forward to desperately snatch at the sheltering bushes that were so very, very near.

You reload on the instant and your eyes are blazing, but the enemy have disappeared. You grin with that terrible thrill of killing men in wartime. You've opened up your battle very well; got three of them in the first surprise before they've had a chance to fire a shot in return or know where your shots came from. They're shaken. They've lost their officer, too. And, though two or three of them may vaguely guess the probable direction the shots came from, they haven't the faintest idea where you are. Your position is still 100 percent; your advantage more so, for you have lessened their number by three.

It is only through using your wits from the very start and by your trained skill in rapid shooting that your position is as it is. You feel a wonderful thrill of confidence and settle down to get the next man.

You have actually done much more than shoot three of the enemy; you have momentarily stopped their advance. They must delay now until they find out the strength of this enemy against them. Somewhere down around that bend there may be an ambush of hundreds of men, thousands possibly. They must find out before they can send word back.

Ah! You see one run crouching from cover to flop down behind a rock. You can see his legs quite plainly, for you quite overlook the little rise up which he is now crawling. You see another man make a dash fifty yards farther to the first man's right. Their object is to crawl warily up that little rise and peer up over the top. You wait awhile; you can clearly see open country ahead of both men; you rightfully decide to wait until they crawl out into that and then you will get them both.

Your eyes are very busy seeking the others; eager to locate each one of the whole twenty-two. If you can, then not only will each man again and again come under your observation but you will know exactly what their plans are, their every move to get you. They will be working on the blind, while you will be able to anticipate their every move ahead. Ah, there's another one just made a dash; they're doing the natural thing, going to work right around your front. This will suit you down to the ground. Over that lower country down there in many places you can see in behind the hills and rises. Many of the little flats are exposed to your view; you can see down into quite a number of the gullies. You estimate that from where they are, to work right around your front until they reach the bend leading away to your left is a good mile. It will take them all afternoon before they can reach the road far to the left and begin to work around you.

Those five away behind up to the ridge are still there, ready to cover their cautiously advancing comrades, if only they could see something to shoot at. They won't see anything to shoot at, for your plans and possy and camouflage are perfect. Presently, they'll begin to fire at your hill. Desultory rifle-fire, a burst from a tommy-gun now and then. They're only trying to draw your fire, trying desperately to locate you. While some of them fire, you know the NCO has his glasses trained on your hill, trying to pick up the puff of smoke when you answer. But you answer only when you're sure of a man.

Ah! Here's one! He runs across a flat and drops down into a gully. He will crawl up that gully to the hill in which it heads and peer out from there. Three hundred yards ahead of where he has disappeared, the gully takes a bend, and that bend is in direct line with you. You can see right down into that bend. You will keep an eye on it, and when he reaches that exposed bend you will shoot him. Carefully you estimate the range of that bend is just on 400 yards.

Ah! Those two fellows you first saw, both are in plain view now, cautiously crawling up the rise. Neither of them knows, of course, that they are under observation. You wait until both crawl well away from cover; you will get both of them. Deliberately you raise the rifle.

"Crack!" One man rolls over in a most surprised sort of way. The other freezes, pressing close to the ground, motionless. He knows that movement will betray him. What he does not know is that your possy completely overlooks his position.

"Crack!" His head and chest jerk up, then sink quietly down. That is five! Five gone from the twenty-five. The original five are still away back, immobilized. They have made no attempt to cross the road away up there; their job obviously is to cover the advancing party. Your flanks apparently are quite safe; you feel utterly confident.

Your eyes are seeking to identify the positions of the twenty men away out there across the road. Each one is a very anxious man. A killer is somewhere near them, a deadly killer; each feels he might stop a bullet any second. They have no idea where that killer may be. They have lost their officer. They are in strange country. They expect a hundred rifles to open out on them at any moment; their ears are anticipating the bark of machine guns; they must press on. But each feels now he may never return, and each crouches down, widely separated from his comrades, hesitating what to do next. The most anxious man of all is their NCO. See if you can pick him out. If you can, you've "got" them.

And so the day wears away; so the fight goes on. Now

and again the sharp crack of a solitary rifle, the deceiving echoes, the silence, and another dead man.

Unless the enemy receives reinforcements, you begin to feel confident you will hold them until nightfall. And then slip away with the news. You wish you had some tiny transmitter to wireless word that the enemy was seeking to penetrate down this hardly known bush track; when you set out this morning, you had not realized how important it might prove.

Through the afternoon, the enemy plane comes back. She roars on down the road, then over the hills to either side seeking, seeking. But she can see nothing. The men below probably have a small wireless and have signalled her that an enemy is holding them up. You do not care whether she drops bombs or not; it's a million to one chance against your being hit.

The plane circles again and again. The observer is as puzzled as the men below. He can see no sign of enemy, and yet he knows from the patrol below that the enemy is there. But he cannot make any guess as to their strength. And he must make sure. He dare not wireless back misleading information that might lead tanks or battalions into an ambush.

You see another chance. "Crack!"—and the fight goes on.

Gradually they work right around your front, but towards sundown there are only half of the original twenty-five left. Suddenly you notice that the covering party has been reinforced; there must be thirty heads now silhouetted along that ridge. Something's doing now!

In the late afternoon shadows you see five men dash across the road away up there to your right. Almost simultaneously, two dash across to the left away down the bend.

You can still hold your position easily; it will be dark before they can work around you. You plan out what to do. Will it be best to wait until dark, hoping for another shot or two at those few men still concealed out to your front, and then quietly slip away when dark comes, or—outflank the flankers? For position is again on your side. You know you are now being outflanked away to both left and right. You can easily withdraw, proceed to outflank the flankers, and get at least two of them.

They still have no idea as to your exact position, or what strength of troops they may at any moment run into. Whereas you know everything.

Perhaps it would be best to slip away now and make back to the nearest troops with all speed. Send news that the enemy is attempting to penetrate down that road. If you got the news through quickly, the nearest military O.C. could hurry troops to the bend during the night. You could direct him to the exact position where a battalion could hold that bend against a brigade.

What would you do?

CHAPTER XII
The Sniper Is Adaptable

In the last two chapters I've given you an incident in a sniper's life that could easily happen again and again in this country. Precisely similar incidents have happened in warfare in other countries. And the Australian continent lends itself to the certainty of such incidents. In Chapters X and XI, I've tried to impress upon you the meaning of what I've written in the preceding nine—the vital importance of cultivating and using your wits. A sniper has not only to be a deadly shot and realize the great value of cover and camouflage, but he *must* cultivate his wits as well. I hope the last two chapters have made clear to you how exceedingly efficient a sniper becomes when he really does that.

Those chapters show, too, that a sniper is not only a lone killer of men, but that circumstances will at times place him in the position of doing a very big job—in the given instance, of holding up the enemy a few vital hours and then rushing news to the nearest military.

If every sniper were equipped with a small, wireless transmitter, it would double his value.

Submachine and tommy-guns are being used more and more in this war. So far it has been, generally speaking, a close-in war. There will be fighting at close quarters, also, when the enemy attempts to invade Australia. But there will be a very great deal of long-range rifle fighting. The very nature of the country will compel that. Which is all the better for the sniper; he can fight both at long range and close quarters. It also makes him more effective, in that he doesn't have to carry the ammunition necessary to keep a tommy-gun in action for long periods. And it gives him greater confidence, because the man armed with a tommy-gun is rarely a deadly rifle-shot.

The Japanese made good use of short-range snipers in Malaya, using them often from the treetops. But the trees and countryside of Australia are very different from Malaya. Doubtless the chance will occur again and again in Australia of a little sniping from trees, but nothing to what will take place on Mother Earth. A perch in a tree grows exceedingly uncomfortable. Again, rarely can the field of fire be compared to that obtainable from vantage points on the ground. Further, once your position is spotted or even suspected, you are practically a goner. You are "tried." They can get all around you and quickly get out of your vision of fire. You have no getaway and but little hope once they catch you up a tree. The treetops and branches may be used occasionally as an auxiliary to ambush by guerrilla fighters, but the tree is by no means an ideal hideout for the lone sniper.

The sniper in trench warfare, however, can use the *artificial* tree to great advantage. This was done to perfection in France during 1916-18. The tree used, of course, had to be in such a position that it commanded the enemy's lines and for some distance beyond. And the trees, of course, were blasted and splintered by shellfire, the branches blown to smithereens so that only the broken trunks remained.

When such a tree trunk, the right size and say about fifteen to twenty feet high, was near enough to a front line, an exact replica of it was made. This had to be a perfect work of art. Behind the lines, a perfect imitation of the tree was built up of sections of bulletproof steel and in shape exactly like the tree. Each cylinder was bolted one upon another. Naturally, the size inside had to be large enough for a man to climb through. Around this "tree," thin iron was beaten out to closely resemble the bark of the tree. Any scars upon it were imitated. The "bark" was then painted to look exactly like the bark of the real tree. As the top of the tree had been blown off by a shell, the imitation was left jagged and splintered, exactly like the original. Up near the top of this splintered stump, a little movable eye slot was cut. A small iron seat and a footrest were fitted in comfortably below it. And a little iron ladder connected these with the ground

When all was ready, one dark night the real tree was quietly pulled down with block and tackle and the dummy erected in its place. The old tree was then removed. A tunnel led from the front line to under the butt of the dummy tree. The sniper would crawl along the tunnel and into the tree. From there, not only could he fire upon the enemy but he was in a position to gather much valuable information.

These "trees" were such perfect imitations that a man could walk past within two feet of one and not realize it was a dummy—unless he tapped it. The damage done to the enemy by snipers in these hideouts was very considerable indeed.

Such camouflage, of course, can only be used in trench and "stationary" warfare. Most of the fighting in Australia may be scattered "wars" of quick movement. Yet, almost certainly, there will be considerable trench fighting. And snipers will be used for "lone wolf" sniping jobs, for sniping with mobile units, and in trench warfare.

If engaged in trench fighting, the sniper chooses, or should be allowed to choose, his own possy. It will be the most advantageous for his purpose. He will make it as inconspicuous and secure as possible. He does the job himself; for if he is to be killed, he does not wish it to be through the fault of some friendly but less expert helper.

This possy becomes his den. He settles down there and carries on his business. His position and loophole or loopholes are constructed so that he has the greatest possible field of fire. Look through an ordinary trench loophole, then through a sniper's. Through the first you probably will see only a small portion of parapet ahead with a glimpse of indistinct country. But the sniper's loophole presents a whole field of vision, a long line of trench with portions of other trenches behind it; a glimpse of the traverses of a communication trench or two; several of what may be more or less concealed enemy observation posts; perhaps also a suspected machine-gun nest. Scanning the local geography, the sniper sees a likely spot which he concludes will probably be used at night as an enemy listening post. (He will get the exact range at his leisure; for by means of a sighted rifle set in a vice or otherwise, the sniper can kill at night, though he does not see a man.) And behind those trenches the loophole still commands a view of quite an expanse of country.

The difference in view between those two loopholes, which may only be a few yards apart, marks the difference between the born sniper and the man who isn't. The one may be a good soldier (the sniper may not, in some sense of the word) and may unerringly shoot an enemy should he get a glimpse of him in his very limited field of vision; the other is an excellent shot with the knowledge or instinct to develop a position from which he can pick off many targets over a far greater area.

On a quiet day, the one may stand by his loophole and not get one shot at a living man. On that same day the sniper may notch in his rifle butt a number of kills.

It is dreadful. But it is war.

A sniper quickly makes his presence felt. Men who become used to a trench, who carry on with daily routine under the usual rifle, machine gun, and artillery fire, move about their duties in more or less lackadaisical manner. But let a sniper start killing—

The news spreads like wildfire. Men at the firing possies now stand by their loopholes with caution, those passing down the trench unconsciously bend the head with a queerly alert expression about the shoulders. When they near some exposed angle where the sniper has killed a man, they bend their backs and hurry past. There is now no careless sauntering, you can see by the expression on their faces what each man is thinking. They build up the parapet, look carefully around (if experienced men) to see if there is any spot over which a bullet might zip in and smack the head of a man passing below. A quite different atmosphere to that when the ordinary daily shooting was going on. An expert is at work now.

All hands try to locate that sniper.

They fail, because their field of vision is similar to that of the first loophole you looked through. Whereas the sniper may be 300, 500, or 1,000 yards away, more even, and at a totally different angle. Even if all those men were staring towards him, his possy is so camouflaged that they would fail to locate him. Otherwise, he would be dead. As it is, he becomes a local menace, levying toll on trenches within range of his rifle for months, and he may never be located. He may not be in a trench at all; he may be concealed up a tree, or away up what looks to be the gnarled, shell-torn trunk of a tree that is really made of painted iron. He may be roosting in a chimney; perhaps in the trench directly opposite, or across to the left or right half a mile away. He may even be firing from directly behind your very own line.

Find the sniper!

Almost impossible. The true sniper is a lone wolf who pits his skill, his cunning, and his life against an entire army. Find him where he hides away out in the open, all alone; pick him out from among his own army, if you can. He is invisible in the open; he is lost in the army. His visiting card is the fatal bullet.

Operating with regular troops in repulsing a landing, scattered among and around the regulars, snipers would cause an enemy especially heavy casualties. They would reap a harvest. The enemy would come packed in boats; thousands of men would leap ashore and charge. The regulars would take heavy toll; the snipers would not miss a shot.

What would be a sniper's value estimated in casualties? That is how friend and foe assess his value. A real sniper, during certain phases of action, might be worth the value of fifty semi-trained men, probably more. Remember, it takes a ton of lead to kill a man. Those fifty men would be firing away their ton of lead, but the sniper would be killing a man at the rate of an ounce per time. Moreover, men behind the lines must keep that ton of ammunition up to those fifty men; and while doing so there must be a certain percentage of casualties. But the sniper seldom becomes a casualty; his job is to make casualties, not become one.

A sniper of the Fifth Light Horse, No. 355, W.E. Sing, accounted for 150 of the enemy in several months at Gallipoli. Long before Sing commenced official sniping, the enemy was securely entrenched so that every target, besides being concealed, had to be first located. The 150 cases are authentic, all witnessed to by an observer using a powerful telescope. Where there was the slightest doubt, it was counted a miss. When the sniper fired alone, as he often did, no hit was recorded. A casualty was counted only when it was clearly witnessed by a trained observer using a telescope. Sing must have knocked many, many more of the enemy.

Thus, beyond any shadow of a doubt, that one man caused 150 casualties to the highly trained enemy within a few months.

What would have been his "bag" had the enemy been untrained men, or had they not been protected by trenches?

I mention this officially authentic instance to show what a deadly man a real sniper is. Multiply this sniper's tally by one hundred. Then think what a thousand such snipers would do to an entrenched enemy in that length of time. Then imagine them shooting at an enemy that was not entrenched. Then assess the value of a brigade of snipers.

Australia possesses the material from which 10,000 real snipers could be trained.

In open combined with trench warfare, and in purely open warfare, the sniper comes into his own. Then comes a real opportunity to utilize to the limit his ingenuity, skill, inborn craft, and daring. He is out in the open, surrounded by the nature which is really part of him. With every bit of nature lending itself to protect him, he is master of every visible target within more than a thousand yards' radius of his rifle-muzzle. Apart from already visible targets, fresh targets are continually popping into view.

The sniper simply melts into his cover. He may be lying within a hundred yards of passing troops and they will not see him. He may be shooting from a thousand yards away, but the only evidence of his presence is the vague "plop" and the deadly bullet. Should the sound eventually be located, a score of men in peril of their lives are detailed to root him out. The sniper expects this. Sees them start after him. Fires leisurely at any further target. Then waits silently. There is nothing to betray his presence.

Each of those twenty men must creep forward over unknown ground; must, sooner or later, show himself. And the sniper claims another victim. When he judges that some of the would-be avengers are nearly outflanking him, he unobtrusively slips away—to select another possy farther back and settle down. Then the plop of his rifle commences all over again.

The sniper's equipment is individualistic but highly modern. He carries an excellent pair of field-glasses. If equipped with glasses not quite to his taste, he seeks an opportunity of securing one from an enemy officer of artillery. He knows that such an officer will have the best field-glasses that the science of the enemy can produce.

In trench or in the open, those field-glasses ally science to the sniper's individual deadliness. They will bring to within a few feet of him objects which even his keen eyes cannot see. With good artillery glasses, you can see the hairs in a man's eyebrows, even when he is peering through a loophole. To the sniper, those glasses, allied to his sniping craft, will even reveal an enemy sniper. His rifle, too, though of the usual military pattern, may be equipped with various sighting aids.

What chance then has the individual untrained soldier against such a man? Even the trained soldier has no chance should he show himself. He need not even do that. Just let the sniper suspect that he is there, or that he is on duty at a certain place at a certain time, or that he is working here or there, and sooner or later the sniper will get or very nearly get him. If he only nearly gets him, that trained soldier takes all possible care that the sniper never gets another chance—at him, anyway.

The respect you gain for a sniper when his bullet smacks within half an inch of your jaw is thrilling.

The idea of the sniper as a strong auxiliary to an army could be developed. In the late war, sniping was only played with, merely an odd man here and there who was an eerie shot and liked to dress himself up as a bush and take phenomenal risks. Then there was that cursed enemy sniper, the fellow who killed so and so and so and so. And we never got him!

Thus it was, by friend and foe. Every nation used the sniper, but as the merest individual sideline, just an odd man or two among every 10,000. I believe the Turks used him more than all the other nations combined.

We vaguely know with what great effect Russia is using her trained snipers. They, and the guerrillas, have played such havoc behind the German lines that they are responsible in no small measure for the tremendous fight put up by the regular Russian armies. When the history of that front comes to be written, there will be honoured chapters given to the guerrillas. And a sniper is one of the most prized members of any guerrilla band.

We read of the Red Army soldier Smolijachkov. He started with 10 men. Trained them to be snipers. The group grew to 300 crack shots. They killed 2,000 of the enemy within three months. And then Smolijachkov was killed. But his band of snipers has carried on; has grown. There are numerous such bands throughout the vast Russian fronts. Imagine the damage they alone have done to the enemy.

We constantly read of the snipers in Africa, China,

Greece, Yugoslavia. The enemy just *cannot* wipe them out. Because, of all fighters, these lone wolves are the very hardest to wipe out.

Brigades of snipers might well develop into the strongest auxiliary of the Australian Forces. No country in the world has such opportunities and human material for sniping as Australia has. Everything points to it; even that strongest thing which breeds the true sniper—the eagerness to be a sniper! Thousands of Australians would glory in it if their homeland was attacked, and thousands of them are snipers born. The Light Horse and snipers are Australia's peculiar national arm.

The main difficulty would be in selecting the men from the rush of recruits. The training would be a work of pleasure to officers, NCOs, and men alike. All that would be needed on the part of the selectors and trainers would be the understanding of the sniper and the art of sniping, together with that sympathy inseparable from the successful formation of first-class sniping brigades.

For the true sniper is not actually, in one sense of the term, a "real soldier." His nature and job and gifts are too individualistic. His duties would vary from the routine duties of the regular soldier; and so his organization and mode of fighting would vary. The regular troops and sniping brigades would have their own distinct jobs to carry out. Working in conjunction, so as to win the maximum fighting power from both, would mean a tremendous addition to Australia's strength.

And now—good luck.

APPENDIX: THE SNIPER
From
The Yellow Joss and Other Tales
by
Ion L. Idriess

Curious how at times, when a man is steadily working, some quite random thought will carry his mind in a flash back years ago.

So it was with me this morning. I was back in the galloping squadrons as we swung under cover behind some low hilly rises during the Gaza-Beersheba stunt. Our squadron hastily dismounted at the extreme end of one of these. A man immediately collapsed with a bullet through his lung. There was a rush to pull the panting horses as close under the sheltering rise as possible, for the dread thought "sniper" flashed through every mind. The enemy was lining the low hills in front of us, but our man had been shot from out on the right flank.

"Crack! Thud!" A horse crashed on its belly as a high-velocity bullet whistled into its flank. "Crack! Thud!" A good-looking chestnut reared surprisingly in the air, pawed frantically in an attempt to regain its balance, then crashed backward to earth, the soft brown eyes growing pitifully big as it struggled gamely to rise.

The trooper/owner stared down at it, intense feeling spreading over his hard, drawn face. A mate rushed out from cover and jerked the man's arm; even as he did so, a vicious, crackling whistle had come and gone. The emu feathers on the trooper's hat fell to his shoulder, sheared clean off to the hat rim.

The anxious squadron crouched close against the rise, each man with his precious horse pulled well in. The sniper evidently could see partly around the extreme corner of the rise, judging by the angle from which the man and the two horses had been shot.

Nothing got more quickly on the nerves of the troops than a sniper. Under several conditions, a thousand men within the range of one solitary sniper could not hit back. Each man simply had to crouch low wherever he was, while the hidden menace systematically picked his targets one by one. That sort of thing on the nerves is ghastly; compared with it, shell-fire is merely in the day's routine.

We felt it intensely that morning. Our brigade was in reserve; at any moment we might be called upon to join in a galloping charge. On the other hand we might have to remain totally inactive for long hours, perhaps all day, with, as far as our squadron was concerned, that searching sniper shooting at our extreme right flank.

Very gingerly I looked from the side of the rise through a pair of splendid field-glasses "souvenired" from an Austrian officer of artillery.

I had the reputation of being a sniper myself. Now, every man knows that when he has built a reputation or has had a reputation thrust upon him, something forces him to try to live up to it, no matter what his heart may be whispering. So I nonchalantly examined the field of barley on our right flank, whence, apparently, the shots had come. But, inside, I knew.

It was a beautiful, sun-kissed field. Emerald-green. The crop was just about a foot high and as level as a billiard table. High in the clear air above the centre of the little field, a brown lark trilled as only larks can. But of life in the field there was not a sign. I knew there would not be. Over every yard, then every foot of its greenness, I searchingly played those high-powered glasses. No slightest depression in the ground, no almost invisible green mound anywhere where green mound ought not to be; absolutely nothing whatever behind, or in, or between which a man could hide. But I well knew that a trained man can lie perfectly still facing you not a hundred yards away on hard, brown earth without even a grass blade on it, and you can stare at the muzzle of his rifle for ten minutes without seeing him. At Enoggera in peaceful Australia, we had been taught this, months before the Landing. And now, somewhere within that field of barley, a highly trained sniper lay easily concealed.

Between us and the edge of the field, just at the foot of the gentle slope which ran down from our sheltering rise, and only a hundred yards away, was a narrow wadi—or gully as we would call it in our own good language. Throwing off haversack and water-bottle, I suddenly jumped from behind the rise and tore down the slope in a crouching run, jerking from left to right, not for three seconds keeping to one straight line. The crackling hisses as the sniper tried to get me by rapid fire were reminiscent of the breath of white-hot iron.

I landed sprawling in the sheltering wadi-bottom and gasped in long, thankful breaths. The first point in the game was won, anyway. I filled my pipe, lit it, and commenced slowly walking up the wadi. The banks were about eight feet high, and I blew the smoke upward so that its dying spirals just cleared the bank and drifted into the air above. When the bank became too high, I pocketed the pipe and doubled back to where I had first sprawled into the wadi.

Pulling barley from the edge of the bank was the next thing; then arranging the foot-long stalks in a row around my hat band and carefully spreading barley in flat sheaves over my back under and over the bandolier and bayonet belt. Each stalk had to be done so very carefully, for if a barley stalk drooped where every stalk should be standing . . . Then came the stealthy climb up the wadi bank and into the barley field. Inch by inch. First the length of the rifle (how heavy the familiar weapon quickly became!) poked gently on ahead, full-length of the arms, through the barley-stalks; then rested gently on the earth, palms of the hands cupped protectingly around the firing mechanism. Then careful craning forward of the head, chin pressed to the ground; then dragging of the entire taut body along by leverage of the elbows. Just one foot advance for each drag, just one inch at a time; chin, chest, belly, and toes pressed tight against the earth while the heart thumped.

A man's mind could *feel* when a single barley stalk, among those through which he crawled, quivered the slightest bit more than it should. Then one long, waiting breath, and, very slowly, on again.

But what a strain on the ears! For it was the ears more than the eyes which might win the next point in this game. Somewhere in that field lay the waiting sniper. Where, I knew not. He would not move. But his eyes would be seeing, his ears would be hearing. And he would shoot.

My mates back on the rise would go through all the old

tricks to attract his fire and attention: a gently-moving hat held just above the skyline with a stick; a rifle poked above a sand mound with a hat slanting on the butt. If this had no effect, a man would dash from cover, then back again, lively—anything so that I might locate the sniper by the crack of his rifle.

So on I crawled, if possible slower and more cautious than before. The further in the barley I was when his rifle cracked, the better chance of locating him correctly. He wouldn't move. From his position, the movement of his eyes alone would naturally show him all up the gentle slope of the rise and around the corner where the squadron was crouching.

If he raised his head the least bit too high above the barley to look for me, he would fall to my rifle, just as I would fall to his should I raise *my* head.

He would simply wait, every instinct, every nerve, every sense tuned to the uttermost with the thrill of longing to put a bullet through my brain. How I understood the feelings of the hidden man, because they were my very own! But his rifle did not crack; he was too cunning a bird to fall to the tricks of my mates. He was waiting for me.

High in the cloudless sky the lark still carolled. From away on the right came a spasmodic crackling, drowned by the fierce, concentrated roar as a brigade burst into sudden rifle-fire. Machine guns butted in with a harsh, metallic chattering. A battery of eighteen-pounders, then two more batteries roared in with a thundering crescendo.

"The En Zeds are into it again," the mind subconsciously whispered. High in the air came the drone of planes. "Our planes are going to lay some eggs!" the mind announced. Then came splitting crashes up in the sky. "Turkish anti-aircraft!" whispered the busy brain. But I saw none of these things, and heard them only as in some other, far-away world. The whole battle today, the battle forever, for me and for him, lay waiting in this peaceful barley field. Though one nation rose and one fell by this evening, it would matter not at all to him or to me.

Without lifting chin from the ground, my eyes would naturally rise slightly to the sky on each pause for breath. Each time they would alight on the carolling lark as it hovered so wonderfully balanced in the air, only to rise almost out of sight in an apparent attempt to sing its way to heaven, to reappear with miraculous rapidity and hover, shrilly singing—and it seemed, as I wormed farther and farther into the field, to hover constantly over one particular spot!

I watched the lark for what seemed a long time; then a breathless realization gripped the mind and tingled through the body until it tautened at the roots of the scalp. I felt my mouth open a little and eyes suddenly widen as I pressed back the rifle safety-catch and gripped hard the splendid weapon. Then twisting very slightly to the left so as to be in line with the hovering lark, I crawled off again. No mother ever nursed her firstborn more gently than I nursed my way through those tender barley stalks that were so easily bruised and swayed.

Sound! What a medley of sound there was! Each stalk harboured life that constantly hummed or hissed or chirped. And things to see! There were countless live things in that barley, some of them swarming over the stalks, things so minute that I never dreamt anything but a microscope could have seen them. And as for the stalks themselves—each had taken on an individual shape; some were tall, some short; some were bent, some straight. Wonderful, too, how far a still man, chin pressed to the ground, could see through that dim, green maze of stalks. Some had wee tufts of grass growing around their butts, and an odd wildflower or two. One scarlet poppy pushed up its crimson cup for sunlight and life. And over all was the song of the lark.

I raised straining eyes, while taking long, steady breaths of the warm earth. How very earthy it smelt! In the air the lark was hovering now, not so very high. At any other time a man could hardly have distinguished that little brown head pointing towards me, now held a little sideways, peering straight down. I wormed a little farther on. Slow, tense minutes passed in withdrawing the field-glasses and carefully raising them just above the ground.

How the barley stalks leapt into prominence! How much farther a man could see! The distance a few yards ahead had before merged into vague greenness; now, far beyond that, one could make out spaces between the barley stalks, and the minute sand pellets around the earthworms' holes looked like brown clods.

Then something moved. It was only the turn of his cheekbone, but it allowed me to focus right into the eyes of my man. Blazing black eyes that had gazed into the haze of the desert seeking the silhouette of the camel caravans many and many a time. Only partly could I see the big brown nose, hawk-shaped, for two twisted barley stalks camouflaged his black *burnous*. The perfectly shaped, tiny black dot of his rifle muzzle I could see, and below the telescopic sight the bony, brown knuckles that gripped around the weapon. A Bedouin, with the eyes of a hawk! How my heart thumped!

As carefully as myself he brought something towards his face. Tilting forward the barley-covered hat, I lay for long minutes, eyelids pressed to the rough earth.

"Field-glasses. Best German make for sure," flashed the racing brain as I lay there motionless—and waited.

At last I raised the head; then slowly, breathlessly,

brought the glasses up again. His eyes now were continually roving in a motionless face, from left to right, from right to left. And I could almost hear him listening!

Very patiently, between all the many barley stalks I concentrated on those two stalks which still crossed his nose. With craning neck I aligned them perfectly, then put the field-glasses gently down while never for the faintest breath of time letting my eyes miss his eyes.

Then the calculation on which one life would depend. Dearly I would have loved to level the rifle foresight fair between those two black eyes—the desire grew almost overwhelming. But many barley stalks besides the two crossed ones were in the way. Such a tiny thing might deflect a bullet—and a man would be allowed only one shot.

I could see the butt of the two stalks as they crossed down his nose in a straight line past the centre of his chin where the black beard hid them.

"Aim right at the butt of the stalks, exactly where the beard covers them. The bullet then should strike that little hollow below the throat at the base of the neck between the two bones and go right down through his body. He should never move after that!"

Then the indrawing of a deep breath, the raising of the rifle, the easing of the racing nerves as the familiar weapon settled its iron-shod butt reassuringly into the hollow of the shoulder; the absolute steadiness as the trigger-finger took the "first pull," and the foresight lowered on the barley stalk down past the eyes, past the mouth, slowly past the chin, until, engaging in the rear sight, it stopped dead where the beard hid the butt of the barley stalk.

"I shall cut that stalk dead in two," whispered the mind in that last fraction of a second of complete steadiness.

"Crack!"

I bounded out of the barley and was on the spot even as he rolled over. He was dying. His flashing black eyes fastened on mine in a gaze of instant realization and deathless hate. He attempted to raise his arm, the sinews tautened in the thick brown wrist as he tried vainly to clench his fist. I knew—he was beseeching all the curses of the Prophet upon this Christian dog who had taken his life. But as his wordless lips bared back in the last of the choking gasps, I only thought:

"I wish I had your splendid teeth, Blackbeard. They are no use to you now!"

Looking down at him, like a great fallen hawk in the crushed barley, I felt no remorse; only hot pride that in fair warfare I had taken the life of a strong man—hot pride that this man, older and stronger physically than I, this man reared from babyhood to regard warfare as the life of a man and splendid sport, this desert irregular knowing every inch of the country, had fallen to a stranger from a peaceful land who knew only three years of war!

Quickly I looked him over for the inevitable souvenirs. Strung on a camel sinew around his neck were thirty-eight identification disks, mostly those of British troops, but with a sprinkling of Australian and one Maoriland badge. A Mohammedan goes to Paradise if he can kill a Christian. So this good religionist had thirty-eight keys to the pearly gates. There was a special silver medal also, and a parchment deed of recognition from the Sultan.

Presently I turned and examined the barley-roots closely. But it was not until a couple of fellows from the squadron came running over that we found what we sought. Within a foot of the Bedouin's body, cunningly interwoven between four stalks of barley, was a little nest, and in it one solitary fledgling, its eyes still shut but hungry mouth wide open. Such an insignificant thing to cause the death of a man!